THE PERON ERA

THE
PERON
ERA

BY ROBERT J. ALEXANDER

NEW YORK

Russell & Russell

COPYRIGHT, 1951, BY
COLUMBIA UNIVERSITY PRESS, NEW YORK
REISSUED, 1965, BY RUSSELL & RUSSELL
A DIVISION OF ATHENEUM PUBLISHERS, INC.
BY ARRANGEMENT WITH COLUMBIA UNIVERSITY PRESS
L. C. CATALOG CARD NO: 65-18783
ISBN: 0-8462-0632-3
PRINTED IN THE UNITED STATES OF AMERICA

TO J.O.P.A.

FOREWORD

༺✿༻

ALTHOUGH THE RISE of Perón and Peronismo is one of the really significant developments in world affairs during the last decade, amazingly little has been written about either the General or his movement. This book is an attempt to make up for at least some of this lack. No attempt is made to write a biography of Perón, but it is hoped that the most important aspects of the development and nature of Peronismo, and something of its significance for Latin America and for the United States are here presented.

Thanks are due to many in this country and in Argentina. In the case of Argentine friends who have provided information and advice, it is better at this time that most of them remain anonymous. However, since Juan Antonio Solari, Secretary General of the Socialist Party of Argentina, is already in such deep trouble with the Perón government that nothing can make it any worse, I can express my appreciation to him for help in meeting people and collecting information while I was in Argentina, and for sending me information since my return.

In this country, I should like to thank Dr. Frank Tannenbaum for reading the manuscript and giving me encouragement, as well as for inciting my original interest in the whole Latin American field. I should also like to mention the great kindness and understanding of Miss Matilda Berg of Columbia University Press, who saw the volume through to publication. Finally, and most of all I want to thank my wife, Joan Alexander, who has extended so much aid—moral, editorial and stenographic—in bringing this little volume to fruition.

ROBERT J. ALEXANDER

Rutgers University
August, 1951

CONTENTS

❧❀❧

CONTENTS

THE PERON ERA

THE STAGE IS SET

❧❦❧

THE RISE of an army colonel to be the idol of the workers of Argentina cannot be understood except against the background of the events of the two decades preceding the military *coup d'état* of June 4, 1943.

Although Argentina has the largest middle class of any country in Latin America, it was not until 1916 that the first "middle class president," Hipólito Irigoyen, was elected by the Radical Party (Unión Civica Radical). Under Irigoyen and his successor, Marcelo T. de Alvear, Argentina experienced perhaps the most democratic period in its history. The Radical regime enjoyed the wide support of the middle classes of Buenos Aires and the provincial cities as well as of much of the working class. Those workers who did not vote for the Radicals voted Socialist, and during this period the Socialist Party more often than not controlled the city council of Buenos Aires, and usually had from half a dozen to two dozen members of the Chamber of Deputies as well as several senators.

Hipólito Irigoyen was reelected president of the Republic in 1928, on the eve of the world depression. Argentina was hard hit by that world-wide catastrophe. In addition, the Radical regime had become increasingly corrupt. The depression and Radical immorality, coupled with the fact that President Irigoyen was then a very old man, formed the backdrop of the Army revolution of September, 1930.

This predecessor of the 1943 coup was engineered by the leaders of the Argentine Army in conjunction with the Conservative, or National Democratic, Party. The Conservative Party is the traditional spokesman for the landowners and has been closely associated with the Church hierarchy in Argentina. The association of the Conservatives and the Army at the time seemed a more logical alignment than the Army-Labor alliance a dozen years later.

Interestingly enough many of the same people who played a leading role in the "labor" administration resulting from the 1943 Revolution were active participants in the pro-Conservative, reactionary uprising of 1930. The general staff of the 1930 revolt included Captain Juan D. Perón, who was in the "operations section"; others were Colonel Juan Pistarini, Air Minister under Perón a decade and a half later, and Lieutenant Colonel Pedro P. Ramírez, president after the 1943 coup. Captain Perón wrote a report entitled "What I Saw in the Preparation and the Revolution Itself," which remains one of the best reports of events leading up to the 1930 revolution.

As president, the revolutionaries picked General José F. Uriburu. He served for two years until, in an election in which the Radical Party was not allowed to take part, General Augustín P. Justo was elected constitutional president. During the administration of Justo the dictatorship was modified and some semblance of democratic constitutional government returned.

However, during no time from 1930 to 1943 was real political democracy restored to Argentina: a fact which helped pave the way for the rise of Peronismo in the 1940's. Although a democratic façade was constructed by Justo and his successors, the great majority of the people were in fact disfranchised. Only in the capital, Buenos Aires, were honest elections held. When by error or oversight an opposition regime was elected in one of the provinces, the Federal government was more likely than not to oust the elected pro-vincial administration and substitute an "interventor" whose purpose it was to hold new elections—and see that they came out "right" the second time.

The country during these years was firmly in the hands of the Conservative oligarchy. Control of the national govern-ment was maintained by various means. The Conservative landowners paraded their peons out to vote for the local Con-servative candidates; when this did not suffice, resort was had to fraud, violence, or "intervention."

The only short break in this shameful record was the two-year administration of President Roberto Ortiz, an anti-Irigoyen Radical who had supported the coup of 1930. He was chosen in 1938 as "front man" for the regime, but after election he refused to front for anyone and began a campaign to restore genuine political democracy to Argentina. He ousted the pro-Nazi Conservative governor of the province of Buenos Aires, Manuel Fresco, and intervened in several of the other more notoriously corrupt Conservative-controlled provinces. His interventors held elections in which the oppo-sition was permitted to win.

However, illness forced Roberto Ortiz to resign after only two years as president. He was succeeded by Vice President Ramón S. Castillo, a faithful old Conservative Party wheel horse who had quite frank pro-Fascist leanings. Castillo pro-claimed for Argentina a highly suspicious "neutrality" in the Second World War and refused to make any move against the blatant attempts by the Nazis and Fascists to terrorize and control the sizable German and Italian populations in Argentina. Moreover, he called off Ortiz's campaign to im-prove Argentine political morality.

Castillo was faced with a hostile congress. The Lower House was controlled by the Radicals and Socialists who made life as tough for the president as they could. An Anti-

Argentine Activities Committee, set up by the Chamber of Deputies, investigated the machinations of the Nazis and Fascists in Argentina. It uncovered fully operating Nazi party networks which were applying pressure on Argentines of German and Italian origin and descent. The Chamber's action served as a warning that the sympathies of the people of the country were with the Allies rather than the Axis, but the Chamber's futility in the face of Castillo's continuing pro-Axis attitude did not help the prestige of democracy in Argentina.

Although personally pro-Franco and pro-Mussolini, Castillo was not representative of the landholder group in this regard. The landowners, whose interests had always been closely tied to British-owned railroads and British markets for wheat, corn, and cattle, were as pro-Allied as any group in the country. So Castillo realistically chose as his successor a leading member of the landed oligarchy, known for his pro-Allied sympathies, Robustiano Patrón Costas. Perhaps the fact that Patrón Costas would almost certainly succeed Castillo in 1944 was one reason for the overthrow of the Castillo government on June 4, 1943, by the far from pro-Ally Army.

The discrediting of democracy by the Conservative regimes from 1930 to 1943 was not the only factor which made possible the rise of Peronismo. Of considerable importance, too, was the change in the nature of the Argentine urban working class. Here two factors had been at work. First of all, there had been an Argentinization of the urban population of the country, and, in the second place, there had been a sizable migration from the countryside into Buenos Aires and some of the provincial cities during the 1930's and particularly after the start of the Second World War.

As a result of the great depression, immigration came to a

virtual standstill and never returned to the 1919–1929 level. The stream of Italian and Spanish workers who had for two generations flooded the cities and pampas of Argentina became a trickle. This meant a fundamental shifting in the political allegiance of the working class of Argentina.

The Spanish and Italian workers who came to the country before, during, and just after the First World War had in many cases taken part in the trade union and political movements of the Old Countries. They were familiar with the ideas of socialism, syndicalism, anarchism then current in their native countries, and they naturally attempted to transplant those ideas and movements to their new home. Thus to a very large degree the Socialists, anarchists, syndicalists who led the labor movement of Argentina during its formative years were immigrants. The radicalism which characterized the early labor movement of Argentina was the result of the influence of immigrant groups, who, of course, won many adherents among native Argentines.

With the passage of time a gradual change took place. More and more of the urban workers were sons of immigrants instead of immigrants themselves. And these second-generation Argentines were above all anxious to prove to themselves, to the rest of the Argentines, and to the world at large that they were "Argentinos." In all too many cases they regarded their fathers' allegiance to anarchism, socialism, syndicalism as part and parcel of "foreignness." Hence, they tended to discard these "imported" ideas and became ready material for some native movement of apparent social reform.

Since there was no longer any great stream of immigration, new workers to man Argentina's growing industries had to come from the hinterland. In the wake of the great depression there was a drive towards industrialization in Argentina as there was throughout the continent, a drive which was intensified as a result of the Second World War. Thus there was a great migration from countryside to city during the 1930's and early 1940's.

These new migrants from the Argentine interior were quite different racially from the older industrial workers, having a much larger admixture of Indian blood than the "porteños" of Buenos Aires. Though the Argentines have a tendency to pride themselves on the fact that they are 95 percent white, this is not strictly true: there are more Argentines with Indian blood in their veins than the figure gatherers are likely to admit.

Culturally, too, these new city dwellers were different from the old. Many more of them were illiterate. All that most of them knew of politics was what they had learned from being marched to the ballot box by their "patrones" to vote for the local Conservative Party dignitary. To them the words "socialism," "syndicalism," "anarchism," "fascism" meant little and indeed were frequently regarded with considerable suspicion as something foreign to Argentina. All that was known of "democracy" was what had been learned from the sad experience with the local Conservative landlords who, quixotically enough, called themselves "National Democrats." As a result, these workers, too, were raw material for a native trade union and reform movement such as was led by Perón after the 1943 revolution.

The old trade union movement had gone through a transformation in the years between the two wars. It no longer was the crusading reform movement it had been before, during, and right after the First World War. In 1922 there had been established the Unión Ferroviaria, a powerful union of the railroad workers. This union and its sister group, "La Fraternidad," consisting of those workers associated with the locomotives, became the pillars of the labor movement. The Unión Ferroviaria developed into a great institution of over one hundred thousand members, with an elaborate social security system which had the aid and blessing of the state. The union had a great deal to lose from any violence or any too great alteration in society.

What was true of the two railroad unions was also more or less true of other important trade union organizations. The leaders became too sure of themselves, perhaps a bit too complacent. And the Socialist Party, to which most of the important union leaders belonged and which might have given inspiration and leadership to the trade unions and kept their eyes on long-range goals, had a policy of not interfering in the internal affairs of the unions. A few of the younger members of the party saw the dangers in some of these organizations and attempted to do something about them.

However, the party was never willing to take a strong position on issues within the labor movement—even when, as in 1942, Socialist Party members were found as leaders on both sides of a split in the main labor organization, the General Confederation of Labor (C.G.T.). In time, indeed, the membership of the trade union leaders in the Socialist Party became largely formal and traditional, and their party membership made but little difference in their behavior as trade union leaders.

These developments within the trade unions had two results. First of all, there was a general lethargy among the rank and file. This is demonstrated by the falling off in attendance at meetings and in the number of meetings held (Table 1). Control of the labor organizations therefore fell more and more into the hands of their leaders and managers.

Against this "bureaucratization" of the labor movement there was considerable revolt, which in the early 1940's was being organized by the Communist Party. The Communists controlled two of the strongest unions in the C.G.T., the metallurgical workers and the construction workers, and were trying to organize other groups including the packinghouse workers. Within the heterogeneous Socialist ranks they found people who were willing to work with them, particularly Angel Borlenghi, head of the Commercial Employees Federation, and Francisco Pérez Leirós, head of the Union of Municipal Workers. Using these two men and their unions as spear-

TABLE 1

Attendance at Union Meetings

(1935 equals 100)

Year	Number of Meetings	Attendance
1935	100.00	100.00
1936	141.64	89.53
1937	126.86	45.04
1938	129.00	45.05
1939	124.96	37.65
1940	108.92	29.86
1941	66.57	20.34
1942	63.65	27.37

heads, the Communists late in 1942 split the ranks of the C.G.T. Two groups were formed, both claiming the name of the old Confederation; they were generally known as C.G.T. No. 1 (the orthodox group, based principally on the Unión Ferroviaria) and C.G.T. No. 2 (the Communist-dissident Socialist group).

This split in the labor movement undoubtedly was a contributing factor to the Army *coup d'état* in June, 1943. Many feel that the coup might never have taken place had the military known that they would face the united opposition of a trade union movement one quarter of a million strong. The unrest demonstrated by the growing Communist strength was also a forewarning of the ease with which the imagination of the rank and file trade unionists might be captured by someone intent on doing so.

Finally, in tracing the background of the coup of June 4, 1943, it should be noted that no government in the preceding twenty years or more had taken any interest at all in the trade union movement and in the working class in general. During his first term, Hipólito Irigoyen had been pro-labor, and his name is still remembered with affection by the Argentine workers. Thereafter, the governments took but little interest in labor's needs and wishes.

This is not to say that there had not been vigorous and valiant fighters for the workers in the halls of Congress. There had consistently been a small group of Socialist Party legislators, sometimes as few as half a dozen, once as many as forty-four (in 1932 when the Radicals were not allowed to run candidates) who fought in favor of working-class legislation. This small group of Socialists, which included such distinguished Argentines as Mario Bravo, Juan B. Justo, Enrique Iberluccea, Nicolás Repetto, and in more recent years Juan Antonio Solari and Américo Ghioldi, had put on the statute books such labor legislation as existed previous to 1943.

However, they were like prophets crying in the wilderness. It was only after the most tenacious fight that they were able to push through meager labor legislation. They had but little encouragement from succeeding Executives, and so far as the presidents were concerned the labor movement was little more than a nuisance.

All of these factors—the discrediting of political democracy, the change of the nature of the Argentine working class, the bureaucratization of the labor movement, the split in the C.G.T., the lack of interest on the part of the succeeding governments in the welfare of the workers—paved the way for the "golpe de estado" by the Argentine Army on June 4, 1943.

JUNE 4 AND AFTERWARDS

§◊§

GENERAL PEDRO P. RAMÍREZ was War Minister in the government of President Castillo. His association with the president appeared to be close, and he was in accord with the position of the government with regard to the war. However, the agreement between the two men was more apparent than real.

For General Ramírez was, in fact, the leader of the movement against President Castillo. A military man of pronounced sympathies with the Axis, General Ramírez was in close contact with a group of Fascist-minded young officers, who in good Latin American tradition had formed a kind of lodge or club known as the Grupo de Oficiales Unidos (G.O.U.). Composed of colonels and lesser officers, the group was quite frank in its sympathies with the Axis in the war and in its avowals of the "manifest destiny" of Argentina in the American hemisphere.

A proclamation of the G.O.U. early in 1943 which was widely circulated in Argentina and abroad after the June 4 coup stated the position of the group very explicitly. It said:

Comrades: The war has shown that it is no longer possible for a country to defend itself alone. The age of nations is being replaced by the age of continents. Yesterday provinces united to form a nation. Today, nations must unite to form the continent. This is the ultimate end of the present war.

Germany is making a titanic effort to unite the European continent. The biggest and best-equipped nation will guide the destinies of the newly-united continent. That nation is Germany.

In South America, there are only two nations sufficiently big and strong to undertake leadership, Argentina and Brazil. It is our mission to make the leadership of Argentina not only possible but indisputable. This task is immense and full of sacrifices. But Germany has given a new sense of heroism to life.

Alliances will be our next step. Paraguay is already with us. We will get Bolivia and Chile. Together and united with these countries, it will be easy to exert pressure on Uruguay. These five nations can easily attract Brazil, due to its type of government and its important groups of Germans. Once Brazil has fallen, the South American continent will be ours. Our leadership will be an accomplished fact.

As in Germany, our government will be an inflexible dictatorship, although at the beginning it may be necessary to make concessions, to entrench ourselves solidly in power.

We must inculcate the masses with the spirit necessary to travel the heroic path on which they will be led. We will do this by controlling the press, movies, radio, books and education, and with the collaboration of the Church.

Our generation will be sacrificed for an ideal—the Argentine fatherland. . . . Viva Argentina!

This young officer element provided the impetus behind the Army coup. The move itself was probably brought on by the proximity of the presidential elections. President Castillo had made it quite plain that he was going to impose a successor of his own choosing on the nation, and this successor was Robustiano Patrón Costas. Patrón Costas owned vast acreage in northern Argentina, and was a symbol of the country's landowning aristocracy. He was, moreover, strongly pro-British, in the tradition of the Argentine cattle and wheat barons. The pro-Axis officers may have feared a shift in foreign policy as a result of the election of Patrón Costas.

The attitude of these young officers is not hard to understand in the light of the fact that since the early 1900's the Argentine Army had been under the training of Germans, that during the 1930's many of its important officers had gone to Germany and Italy for study and had there been indoctrinated in the ideas of the Nazi and Fascist military cliques, and had become convinced of the invincibility of the Axis powers. This indoctrination had certainly not been overcome by the middle of 1943 by any conviction that an Allied victory was inevitable.

The overthrow of the constitutional president was organized principally by the Campo de Mayo garrison a few miles outside of Buenos Aires. With masterly precision, the troops from Campo de Mayo marched on the capital and occupied it in the early afternoon of June 4, 1943. They surrounded the Casa Rosada, the Argentine White House, but President Castillo had already fled Buenos Aires on a gunboat. He later returned and was allowed to retire to his private home, where he died four months later.

President Castillo was succeeded by General Arturo Rawson, a part of the drama not in the script. It had been agreed by all concerned in the movement that the new provisional president should be War Minister Ramírez. However, the leader of the troops which actually marched on Buenos Aires was General Rawson, so, taking advantage of the situation when announcing from the balcony of the Casa Rosada the resignation of President Castillo, he proclaimed himself the new provisional chief executive.

President Rawson's term lasted only two days. The leaders of the revolt finally brought him to reason and he resigned. He was soon appointed ambassador to Brazil, a largely decorative post which he held for some time, becoming more and more opposed to the regime. He later returned to Argentina, only to stand trial, be exonerated, and pass on to the oblivion of retirement. And so ended the tragicomic side of the June 4 revolt.

Meanwhile, the new government met with a mixed reception. There were many who felt that Castillo was so bad that a change could only be for the better. Later the Peronistas were to claim that this was the universal attitude. There were others who proclaimed with some positiveness that the military had overthrown Castillo because of his pro-Axis attitude and that the new regime intended to enter the war on the side of the Allies. The United States government apparently had some reason for thinking that this was the truth, since the Ramírez regime was recognized a week after it seized power.

However, many Argentines were less sure of the pro-Allied and democratic intentions of the new administration. The leader of the Socialist Party, Nicolás Repetto, who was then in the United States, on the day after the revolt gave a statement to the press in which he pointed out that the leaders of the new regime were, if anything, more pro-Axis than Castillo.

For the most part the people and their leaders took a "wait and see" attitude toward the military government, and it was not long before its intention became quite clear. The regime began to take steps which even Castillo had not dared to initiate. It dissolved Congress, which had been such a thorn in the side of President Castillo and the only real spokesman for the mass of Argentine voters.

The new regime moved against the labor unions. It decreed the dissolution of the C.G.T. No. 2, headed by Francisco Pérez Leirós and backed by the Communists, on the grounds that it was a Communist organization. At about the same time the government decreed the ousting of the elected leaders from three of the country's principal labor unions, the Unión Ferroviaria, La Fraternidad, and the Union of Municipal Workers (Pérez Leirós's own union). In place of these organizations' elected officials, the military government appointed military officers.

C.G.T. No. 1 was badly disorganized. Those of its affiliates which had been "intervened" withdrew temporarily from all activity in the Confederation, and the C.G.T. transferred its headquarters from the building of Unión Ferroviaria to that of Unión Tranviaria, the trolley-car workers' union. The secretary general of the C.G.T. No. 1, José Domenech, resigned his position in protest.

C.G.T. No. 1 issued a statement which said in part:

What has happened is an incident like others through which the labor movement has passed, and will serve to awaken new energies in the working-class, which, purged and reorganized, will become a greater power in the destiny of the Nation. It is hoped that the incident will be purely temporary and that the intervened organizations will soon recover their liberty of action and rejoin the Confederation. Furthermore, the workers hope that the government . . . will adopt no further measures likely to damage the workers.

Meanwhile there was difficulty in the "intervened" unions. A naval captain was the first choice as "interventor" in Unión Ferroviaria, but he immediately stirred up a hornet's nest of intra-union politics in the organization, and the military government soon found it necessary to replace him. His successor was Lieutenant Colonel Domingo Mercante, who continued to run the organization as long as it was under the government's control.

As the months passed, the Ramírez regime created more and more trouble for itself and the country. It soon became evident that Ramírez and his friends had no intention of joining the Allied cause in the war, and if anything were more violently anti-Allied than was Castillo. Groups which had been organized to rally support for and give aid to the Allies, such as the Junta Feminina Para la Victoria and Acción Argentina, were closed by the government, while pro-Axis groups remained untouched.

Several of the government's moves within the country tended to unite a large part of the population against it. In September alone, over seventy papers were suspended for criticizing the regime. Late in December, 1943, the government decreed the reinstitution of Catholic religious instruction in the public schools. This question had been a dormant one for half a century; in 1884 the issue had been fought and won by the forces in favor of a secular public school system. The military regime, in a move apparently designed to win the support of Church hierarchy, now suddenly reestablished compulsory Catholic instruction in the schools supported by the Federal government—which included most of the country's educational institutions.

Two other decrees were published late in December to take effect on January 1, 1944. The first of these outlawed all political parties, and their headquarters were occupied by the police. In some cases the move was anticipated, and before the police arrived all vital records, including membership lists and other "incriminating" material, had been removed from the files.

The second measure established what was perhaps the most stringent press control in the country's history. A number of papers and periodicals, including the Socialist daily paper *La Vanguardia,* ceased publication rather than submit to the new regulation.

The democratic parties of Argentina were thus forced underground. The stories which the underground leaders tell match some of those emanating from Europe at the same time. For the most part, the leaders of this Argentine underground were utterly unfamiliar with such a type of operation. They indeed got many of their ideas from books they had read and movies they had seen about similar situations in the occupied countries of Nazi-dominated Europe.

In the case of one of the underground groups, the form of

organization was cellular, with three members to each cell. These three knew one another, but did not know members of other cells. The leaders of the organization were five in number; each had a substitute whom he personally named and who would take his place in case of necessity. One of these leaders did most of the writing for underground publications. He was the only one who knew where to deliver the material to the printers, but he did not know where the printing press was or who worked there. Nor did he try to find out.

The printing plant was the heart of the whole underground setup. The principal press of this group was seized by the police, who announced triumphantly that now this malicious propaganda would cease. The same day a new issue of the same paper appeared.

The underground publications were many in number. Some were mimeographed; others were printed, with thousands of copies of each issue. Sometimes special items were circulated, such as Ramírez's resignation as president in February, 1944, which was never published by the government but which the underground received word of and printed. Copies of all publications were always sent to the leading government people, the police, the military, and to the foreign representatives in Buenos Aires.

Sometimes public demonstrations of opposition to the regime were made. In October, 1943, over one hundred and fifty leaders in politics, labor, industry, education, and social affairs signed a Manifesto for Democracy, demanding a return to constitutional government. Circulated throughout the country, the manifesto evoked wide support. All those signing it who had teaching positions or any other government posts were immediately dismissed.

Students were particularly active in conspiratorial work during these months. Their organizations were in united opposition to the regime, and student strikes were frequent and bitter. The student groups were in direct contact with certain elements in the Army. Upon several occasions the students and dissidents among the military were willing and anxious to try violent action against the regime, but the political leaders would not agree to do so.

The regime exiled and jailed hundreds of its opponents. Among those who sought refuge in Montevideo, the Uruguayan capital across the Rio de la Plata from Buenos Aires, were leaders of the Radical, Socialist, Communist, Progressive Democratic, and National Democratic parties. From there they carried on continuous agitation, publishing newspapers and other documents which were smuggled into Argentina for wide distribution there. They also carried their campaign against the *de facto* regime to the radio, broadcasting on local Uruguayan stations that could be heard easily in Argentina.

Concentration camps were established in the region of Patagonia and Tierra del Fuego. Many dissident trade union leaders, especially Communists, were sent there. Other opponents of the regime were held prisoner in the Villa Devoto penitentiary outside of Buenos Aires, while still others were kept in local jails for a longer or shorter period of time.

It was not until early in 1945 that the oppressive measures were relaxed. In preparation for the presidential election, finally held in February, 1946, the government permitted the return of the exiles, emptied the concentration camps and jails, and permitted the press to function once again with comparative freedom. However, by that time, great changes had occurred in the government itself—changes which are the story of the next chapter.

PERON TURNS TO THE
LABOR MOVEMENT

෯

HIGH IN THE COUNCILS of the new regime was Colonel Juan Domingo Perón. An officer in his late forties, Perón had spent a number of years abroad, including some time in Fascist Italy, where he had studied the tactics of the Duce's Alpine troops. He had played a significant role in the Army coup of 1930, and he was soon to loom as the most important man in Argentina as a result of the 1943 revolution.

Perón was born on October 8, 1895, in a small town south of Buenos Aires. He is said to be the great-grandson of an Italian senator named Peroni, who migrated to Argentina from the island of Sardinia. At the time of Juan Domingo's birth his father was a small farmer. Hard times struck the Perón family and, when Juan was still a very young boy, his father moved to Chubut in cold and rugged Patagonia, where he worked for some years as a hired hand. Later the family settled near Commodoro Rivadavia, the oil port in the southern part of the province of Buenos Aires where the elder Perón bought a sheep ranch. This ranch is still in the family.

Young Juan Domingo Perón entered the National Military Academy, from which he graduated without any particular distinction. He was commissioned a sub-lieutenant at eighteen and became a full lieutenant at the age of twenty. His subsequent Army career was not spectacular. He took advanced training, taught for a while in the National Military Academy, and wrote several books on military strategy, though he had no occasion to put his teachings into practice. His chief distinction was as a fencer and he was at one time the foils champion of the Argentine Army.

One of Perón's unofficial activities was participation in the Grupo de Oficiales Unidos (G.O.U.). He took a leading part in its deliberations, and there are those who maintain that he was its chief inspirer and leader.

His first wife, whom he married early in his career, died in 1938. Their adopted daughter is now a grown woman living in the provincial city of Mendoza.

At the time of the 1943 Revolution, Perón was in the prime of life. He was six feet tall, handsome and particularly attractive to women. His fairly large head was topped by dark, sleek hair which he brushed straight back from his forehead, accentuating his height. His nose was aquiline and his eyes close-set and black-brown in color. He had a florid complexion, induced by a network of veins running close under the skin of his cheeks.

As events were to show, this Colonel Perón was a man of unbounded ambition and a sense of mission. He was an exceedingly hard worker, who rose early, was at his office by seven o'clock in the morning and often stayed there until eleven o'clock at night. He was a man with a magnetic personality which impressed even those who disagreed completely with him or who disliked his politics intensely. His ability to convert visiting newspapermen, officials, or foreign dignitaries to his point of view soon became famous.

As he was to demonstrate, Perón was—and remains—a man of great personal charm. He is described by Sumner Welles as being both "guapo" and "muy macho"—brave and very masculine—qualities which are particularly appealing in Argentina. In the course of his political career, Perón was to assume a democratic air, complete with warm smile, which made him seem as comfortable in shirt sleeves among a group of "descamisados" as one would expect him to be among a group of Army officers.

Opinions differ concerning the Argentine leader's oratorical powers. Some foreign observers find his voice rasping; others, like Milton Bracker of the New York *Times*, assert that "his primary appeal is in his voice." In any case he is capable of bringing a group of Argentine workers to the highest peak of emotional tension and arousing in them a passionate loyalty —even in the sophisticated "porteños" of Buenos Aires.

With the advent of the military government, Colonel Perón became chief of the secretariat of the Ministry of War and president of the National Labor Department. The latter organization was notoriously ineffectual and both employers and workers tended to have as little to do with it as they possibly could. It was not equivalent to a Ministry of Labor; its president did not have ministerial status and had in the past been appointed from lesser members of the political machine in power. It is not impossible that when he first took over his position, Colonel Perón did so merely because the job had to be given to someone, and it seemed a position which would involve comparatively little trouble.

For the first few months of the regime, Colonel Perón was heard of only infrequently. However, he and a few of his particular friends were observing the trend of events very closely. Perón and his circle, which included his nominal superior, Minister of War Edelmiro J. Farrell, and the interventor in Unión Ferroviaria, Colonel Mercante, soon came to realize that the tack which the military regime was taking was a wrong one. They saw that the highhanded measures of the Ramírez administration were serving no purpose except to alienate most of the country's politically active population. Perón and his friends came to the conclusion that if the regime were to have any serious chance of survival, it would have to find a popular base.

Perón and Mercante in the course of their jobs had come into close contact with the labor movement. In their search for popular support it was but natural that they should turn to those with whom they were in day-to-day contact. A series of meetings took place between the Perón military group and some of the country's leading trade unionists. Among those who sat in on these sessions were Juan Bramuglia, then lawyer for the Unión Ferroviaria, and others of that union, leaders of C.G.T. No. 1, and Angel Borlenghi and José Argaña of the Commercial Employees Confederation, while on the military side the participants included Perón, Farrell, Mercante, and Colonel Velazco, a member of the Army General Staff, and later head of the all-powerful Federal Police.

The soldiers asked the trade unionists what they wanted. The labor leaders answered cautiously at first. However, soon they were naming all the things the unions had been vainly seeking for years: freedom for labor to organize throughout the republic; a Ministry of Labor which would really function; a pension system for the Commercial Employees; some new hospitals for the social security system of the Unión Ferroviaria. They also advised the military men to end the "intervention" which the revolutionary regime had instituted in various unions.

After listening to the trade unionists, Perón and his friends proceeded to offer jobs to the labor leaders participating in the discussions. These were refused, but the labor leaders agreed to continue to consult with the military, to offer them suggestions, to tell them whether labor considered their actions good or bad. For the moment, this was as far as they would go in offering their support to the *de facto* government.

Soon after these discussions, the Perón group within the government began their two-year campaign to rally working-class support. The old Department of Labor was converted into the Secretariat of Labor and Social Welfare. It became virtually a ministry, although it could not have this title since the Constitution forbade the establishment of any new ministries. Colonel Perón became the first Secretary of Labor and Social Welfare and Juan Bramuglia was made his chief assistant as Director General of Labor. Subsequently, with the ousting of Ramírez as president, and his replacement by General Farrell, Colonel Perón took on the added jobs of Minister of War and Vice President.

The Secretariat of Labor, however, remained the key to Perón's rise to power, and his activities in that ministry were manifold. During his tenure of office as secretary a large volume of labor legislation was put on the books. Before this time, Argentina had had only rudimentary beginnings of a social security system. One or two of the stronger unions— outstanding among them the Unión Ferroviaria—had succeeded in getting social security institutes set up to cover their members. However, there was no general social security system, and only a small proportion of the workers were covered.

During 1944 and 1945, Perón established by decree social security institutes covering virtually all the country's workers. Separate funds were set up for white collar workers, industrial workers, agricultural workers, maritime workers, and several other categories. Finally, in 1945 the system was rounded out with the establishment of a National Institute of Social Security of which all individual funds became component parts. As a result, Argentina was converted from the most backward country in South America in social insurance matters to one of the most advanced.

In other fields, too, the Secretariat of Labor was active. In December, 1943, half a billion pesos was appropriated for the construction of low-cost housing. Early in 1945 a decree was issued providing that all persons working for hire were to get ten consecutive days of annual vacation with pay after one year of service, and fifteen days after five years.

Pressure from the Secretariat brought wage increases in many fields. Some years after Perón became president, the Secretary General of the General Confederation of Labor, José G. Espejo, gave out figures which indicated that the average worker's wage increased from 1,700 pesos a year in 1943 to 3,900 pesos in 1948, and that the average daily wage increased from seven pesos to sixteen. He maintained that wages went up a good deal faster than prices during this five-year period. He said that the increase in wages in the period 1943 to 1948 was 241 percent, while the cost of living during the same period rose 167 percent. There is no doubt some exaggeration in Espejo's figures and they cover a longer period than did Perón's tenure as Secretary of Labor. However, since wages probably went up a good deal faster between 1943 and 1945 than they did in the subsequent period, Espejo's figures give some indication of the magnitude of the wage increases brought about while Perón was Labor Secretary.

Perón began to gather into his own hands as much of the machinery of collective bargaining as possible. Unions and employers were invited to bring their problems to the Secretariat. It soon became evident that, more often than not, negotiations conducted there resulted in sizable concessions to the workers. These new collective agreements were given the widest possible publicity. Pictures of the successful conclusion of contract negotiations showing Colonel Perón in the middle, with representatives of the workers on one side and representatives of the employers on the other, became common. Workers soon began to feel that the man in the middle was more important than the union leaders in the outcome of these negotiations—which was the impression which Perón desired to give them.

On the other hand, what happened to those who would not use the Secretariat of Labor as a medium for collective bargaining was illustrated by the case of a strike of the Grafa Company workers. Several hundred were arrested and all the workers were forced back to their jobs. On this occasion, Perón said:

We represent justice in labor matters. One must accustom oneself to the idea in the same manner that sensible persons have accustomed themselves to go to the police and the courts. To those who refuse to recognize the labor authorities will happen the same that happens to those who attempt by force to take justice into their own hands. These workers of Grafa have placed themselves in that situation, and we, charged with the governmental function of avoiding, preventing and resolving everything that might signify a threat of economic disturbance, have declared illegal the movement which did not consult us, and summoned the workers to return to work.

Perón's influence helped many workers in their organizing activities. For example, in the packinghouses union organization had hitherto been virtually impossible. For a short time after the First World War a union had been established in the principal packing plants, but it had been destroyed as the result of irresponsible anarchist leadership of a walkout. A second attempt was made twenty years later, in 1939, this time under Communist auspices, but by 1943 there was little left of this organization. Attempts to organize were met by the firing of all union members. The companies maintained elaborate spy and police systems in order to thwart unionization. Some union leaders were even murdered. Meanwhile the workers labored long hours at poor pay and were subject to a variety of petty tyrannies at the hands of foremen and company officials.

In September, 1943, a general strike occurred in the packing plants around Buenos Aires. Thousands of workers went out, there was considerable violence and several deaths resulted. However, for the first time the workers found that they had the support of the government. Through Perón's influence the companies and the union were finally brought together to sign the first collective bargaining contract in the industry.

Perón himself visited the packinghouse town of Berisso. He walked down the main street with his arm around the shoulders of Cipriano Reyes, the leader of the local packers' union. No doubt remained that the meat packers' unions had the official endorsement of the most powerful man in the military government. No longer would it be possible to accuse the union leaders of being "anarchists" or "Communists."

From these first organizing efforts there grew one of the most important trade unions in Argentina, the Federación de la Industria de la Carne y Afines. This union remained outside of the C.G.T. and continued to be one of the most militant and forthright organizations in the labor movement—and one of the chief sources of strength for Colonel Perón, as he was to find out on October 17, 1945.

In semitropical northern Argentina it had been virtually impossible to establish labor unions before 1943. The big landowners and employers *were* the government. They had their own private police forces and deported, jailed, and tortured labor organizers and union members. The Perón Revolution changed all this. For the first time, some of the most oppressed and backward workers were able to form unions. In the province of Tucumán, Perón personally helped organize a Federation of Sugar Workers which became the nucleus for a strong provincial federation of labor.

In the older centers of union activity, groups which had never had an interest in unionization, or which perhaps had never even heard of unionism, were brought into the trade union movement. In the provincial city of Mendoza, a priest,

Padre Luis Dante Picconi, acting on the basis of propaganda from the Secretariat of Labor in favor of trade unionism, began early in 1944 to organize trade unions, beginning with a group of trolley-car workers. In the succeeding months he organized twelve new unions, including intercity bus drivers, local bus drivers, employees of various wineries, road mainte-nance workers, and wood sellers. These groups had the back-ing of the Secretariat of Labor, which prevented the employ-ers from penalizing workers who took part in union activities. For most of these workers, trade unionism in Argentina be-gan with Juan Domingo Perón.

The older unions grew rapidly. Membership in the Unión Tranviaria (trolley-car workers) grew from 9,000 to 28,000 in three years and spread from Buenos Aires to most of the im-portant provincial towns and cities. Even the Unión Fer-roviaria, which was already the country's largest trade union, increased its membership by 25 percent. Other groups grew at a greater or lesser pace.

The Secretariat of Labor came to have an increasing amount of influence in the labor organizations themselves. As the Secretariat began to expand social legislation and to aid the unions in various ways, many old-line trade union leaders began to change their attitude toward the govern-ment. They began to compliment the Secretariat on this act and the other. It was not long before the support of union members began to be transferred from the old trade union leaders to Perón. In fact, the old-line leaders themselves built up the "mystique" of Perón. Some of them quite frankly ad-mitted later that by the time they realized what they had done, Perón had taken their followers out from under them, and there was little they could do to alter the situation.

The change was most notable in the case of the General Confederation of Labor (C.G.T.). The Confederation was very badly disorganized. First there was the split of December, 1942, and then the withdrawal of the Unión Ferroviaria and La Fraternidad at the time the government took over these unions. For a while the leadership of what remained of the C.G.T. remained officially opposed to the military regime and to Colonel Perón himself.

The first major test came in May, 1944. The government proposed that there be a patriotic demonstration on the country's Independence Day, May 25, which would in essence be a demonstration in favor of the government and its policies. An invitation to the C.G.T. to participate started a battle royal within the ranks of the Labor Confederation. The pro-government group finally won, with the result that the anti-government elements resigned from the Central Committee of the C.G.T.

In August there was another crisis. The C.G.T. organized a meeting in support of the "neutral" foreign policy then being followed by the regime. This meant a complete reversal of the C.G.T.'s pro-Allied position. Again there was a knock-down, drag-out fight within the ranks of the C.G.T., but once more the pro-government forces were victorious. The position of the Confederation was clearly stated by the organ of the Labor Confederation, *C.G.T.*, when it published an article declaring the organization's support of the *de facto* military regime of Farrell and comparing the C.G.T.'s position with that of Spanish trade unionists of the 1920's who found it possible to support the dictatorship of Primo de Rivera.

This article brought forth a futile protest from the remaining anti-Perón elements in the C.G.T. After this incident, the anti-Peronistas virtually ceased all activity in the organization. In September, 1945, the textile workers, shoemakers, and La Fraternidad (which had reentered the Confederation early in 1945 when government intervention in the union ended) withdrew from the C.G.T.

The Peronistas now moved to consolidate as much of their

labor strength as possible in the General Confederation of Labor. Unions which had taken part in the C.G.T. No. 2 were brought back into the officially recognized—and controlled —C.G.T. Most of the new unions springing up as a result of the booming organizing activities were also brought into the C.G.T. Even some old unions which had never been in the C.G.T. entered the Confederation. One of these was the Federation of Telephone Workers, which had been organized and headed by Luis Gay, a syndicalist who was now won over to support Perón.

Good jobs were used as bait to lure undecided labor leaders into the Perón camp. A list was made of all the influential unionists in the country; opposite each name was written the job for which he might sell his support. The man the Peronistas most desired to enlist was José Domenech, who had been secretary general of the C.G.T. before the June 4 revolution and who resigned in protest against the intervention by the government in the Unión Ferroviaria. He was told to pick whatever job he desired: to their dismay he refused.

Many of the new jobs were in the Secretariat of Labor. Most of the fourteen provincial "delegations" of the Secretariat were headed by old trade unionists. In the home office there was a corps of "trade union advisers" to the Secretary, each of whom drew a good salary, but none of whom seemed to have any very specific duties. There were other administrative positions in the rapidly expanded Secretariat. Later, in the election campaign of February, 1946, trade union leaders rode on the Perón ticket to membership in the national legislature and in provincial legislative bodies. Three of the principal Peronista labor union leaders were rewarded with cabinet posts when Perón became president.

It is said that where bribes would not work, blackmail was not scorned. One labor leader who had unintentionally committed a criminal act was threatened with exposure and prosecution if he refused to support the government. He became a "loyal" Perón man.

To consolidate firmly its control of the labor unions, the government introduced in October, 1945, a strict new regimen. From that time forward, if a union wanted to sign a valid collective bargaining contract or wanted to make use of the facilities provided by the Secretariat of Labor it would have to be registered with the government and be granted "personería gremial"—legal recognition. The decree further provided that only one union should receive "personería gremial" in any industry or trade in any given region and that the favored union would be the one with the majority of the workers.

With this weapon, Colonel Perón and his successors in the Secretariat of Labor were able to destroy most of the few remaining unions of importance which refused to surrender to the government. Two of the most important of these "recalcitrants" were the National Shoe Workers Union and the Textile Workers Union. Both of these groups were headed by Socialists, had withdrawn from the C.G.T., were in outspoken opposition to the government-controlled unions, and were the principal organizations in their industries.

The National Shoe Workers Union, organized as a national body in 1917, had at the end of 1945 a nation-wide contract with the principal organization of shoemaking employers. As soon as the decree regulating unions was published, the union made application to be recognized and granted "personería gremial" under the edict. No answer was received from the Secretariat concerning this request, and the union was informed by the Secretariat that its leaders were unwelcome there.

In a few weeks a rival shoemakers' union made its appearance, headed by men who had been expelled from the National Shoeworkers Union on charges of being allies of the employers. These men now avowed their friendship for the government and for Colonel Perón, and within a short time their new union was granted "personería gremial."

It was not until March, 1946, however, that the fate of the National Shoe Workers Union was finally settled. At that time the union's national contract with the employers expired and the union informed the employers that it desired to negotiate a new agreement. The employers were willing, but the Secretariat of Labor called in the union leaders and informed them that they had no right to enter into negotiations since they did not have "personería gremial," and that the rights of negotiation now rested with the rival group. The employers were similarly notified. They were divided on the issue, the majority agreeing to go along with the government's dictum, a smaller group continuing to bargain with the old union. The net result of this whole incident was that the National Shoe Workers Union lost virtually all of its members, since it was no longer legally empowered to bargain in their name.

A similar procedure was followed in the case of the Union of Textile Workers. The organization was denied legal recognition, a rival Association of Textile Workers was established, was immediately recognized by the government, with the result that it was then empowered to conduct collective bargaining negotiations. Both of the new Peronista unions joined the C.G.T.

OCTOBER 17th

֍

ALTHOUGH the *de facto* government had been in power for more than two years, it did not enjoy a particularly strong position as the last quarter of 1945 began. The regime had not yet achieved what is the fond desire of every revolutionary administration in Latin America—to transform itself into a "constitutional government." The military had wagered incorrectly on the outcome of the war, and although it had hastily turned coat and declared war on the Axis powers just a few days before the deadline set at Yalta, Argentina was in a position of isolation which had scarcely been equaled in the country's history.

Opposition to the regime was still strong and active. With the lessening of the reins of the dictatorship early in 1945, in preparation for the presidential election of February, 1946, the opposition had once again become vocal and was succeeding in rallying a good deal of support. In June a manifesto was issued by 321 industrial and commercial organizations, attacking the social and economic policies of the regime and denouncing Vice President Perón in particular. Among the signers were the Argentine Rural Society, the Rural Society of Rosario, the Argentine Industrial Union, and the Argentine Rural Confederation—the most important spokesmen for landlord and management interests.

The state of siege, which had been in effect since Pearl Harbor, was lifted late in August. This paved the way for the

largest demonstration which the opposition had made since
the coming to power of the *de facto* government. This was the
so-called "March for the Constitution and for Freedom" on
September 19, 1945. During this mammoth demonstration
and parade through the main streets of Buenos Aires over
400,000 people took part and all elements of the opposition
were present. At the head of the marchers were leading figures
from all walks of life and from all political groups opposed to
the regime.

It was freely predicted that this great outpouring of the
opposition forces spelled the beginning of the end of the *de
facto* regime, and in particular the downfall of Colonel Juan
Domingo Perón. The worried government bestirred itself: a
few days after the "March for the Constitution," the state of
siege was once more slapped on the country. Even before this
modified form of martial law went into effect, the government
rounded up many of the principal leaders of the opposition.
In this greatest manhunt in Argentine history, Colonel Perón
himself was in active charge. Arnaldo Cortesi tells of this
incident:

. . . Peron sits behind a huge flat-topped desk between two
windows, looking out upon the gardens and fountains of the
historic Plaza de Mayo.

He seizes the telephone and gives the chief of police instructions
about several hundred arrests he wants made. "No, a state of
siege is not yet in force," he is heard to say, "but you go ahead
and bring in all the persons on the list."

Shortly afterwards the first reports begin to come in. "You've
got Dr. Gainza Paz of La Prensa? Good. Now make sure you get
Dr. Luis Mitre of La Nación. What? Dr. Peralta Ramos of La
Razón got away? How did that happen? All right, now, get busy
on the rest."

. . . By telephone, by wire, by messenger reports keep pouring
in not only from the city of Buenos Aires but also from the provinces. No detail seems too small to deserve his personal attention

and he finds time also to spur on the police to even greater efforts. Not one of the men and women who have dared to stand in his way is to fail to see the inside of a jail before the day is over. At last, late at night, he moves to police headquarters to look over the day's haul of prisoners in Buenos Aires.

Violence continued for several weeks after the reimposition of the state of siege on September 26. A general strike of university students was called on October 4 to protest the attacks by the police on student organizations. The police broke into La Plata University, routed the students and arrested Vice Rector Cibelli.

The next day the police closed the newspaper *La Crítica* and broke up a women's rally in protest against the state of siege. Eighteen hundred students were held by the police. The Argentine Medical Association resolved to call a general strike of doctors, while the physicians associated with the Railroad Workers Hospital refused to attend a ceremony in honor of Colonel Perón.

Finally, on October 9, 1945, the Army garrison at Campo Mayo, just outside of Buenos Aires, rose in revolt. They were led by the post commander, General Eduardo J. Avalos, who had been in contact with the anti-Peronista students and other groups opposed to the Colonel. Avalos, one of the chief leaders of the June 4th movement, was not regarded as a democrat, but he was a jealous rival of Perón. When approached by the younger members of the officer corps of Campo de Mayo, Avalos seized his opportunity and undertook the leadership of the anti-Perón movement.

Perón had apparently gotten wind of Avalos's negotiations and had planned to exile him to some far distant outpost. However, the officers of the Campo de Mayo backed Avalos and, thus encouraged, he refused to yield, but instead led a march on Buenos Aires. On the way, his group was intercepted by aviation troops from near-by Palomar airfield; they were loyal to Perón and were determined to halt the march. Before any clash occurred, negotiations were held and Perón was persuaded to resign from all of his posts.

Perón himself commented on the cause of these developments when he wrote several years later:

If . . . serious difficulties arose during the period of the "de facto" government it was due to the inevitable fact . . . that . . . the interpretation and aims of a revolution are not identical even among the revolutionaries themselves. I can speak about this because, besides other manifestations that are of public knowledge, those differences brought about my separation from the government and confinement on the Island of Martín García.

The next day, October 10, Perón made an appeal for labor support in this moment of crisis. His speech from the balcony of the Labor Secretariat was broadcast over the official government radio network.

Becoming bolder, the Campo de Mayo group then insisted on October 12 that Perón be placed under arrest and that all of the ministers and secretaries of state resign except Avalos, who had had himself appointed war minister in Perón's place, and R. Sustaito, the new minister of air. On the same day a two-man cabinet was formed. It consisted of General Avalos, who became Minister of Foreign Affairs and Minister of Interior as well as of War; and Vice Admiral Héctor Vernengo Lima, who was named Minister of Navy, of Finance, and of Justice and Public Instruction.

The new government moved swiftly to undo many of the acts of the Perón administration. All university and school teachers who had been ousted for opposition to Perón were ordered reinstated; the Organic Statute on Political Parties (decreed in preparation for the presidential election and denounced as highhanded and undemocratic by the opposition) was rescinded; it was resolved to hold the forthcoming elections under the electoral law in existence before 1943. The Propaganda Division was dissolved, the Director General of the Subsecretariat of Press and Information was dismissed, and freedom of the press was restored. The Communist Party was legalized. All political prisoners were released and a Federal judge in Córdoba province, who had been removed for displeasing Perón, was reinstated. All universities were reopened.

Despite the new government's moves to liquidate the dictatorship, the civilian politicians refused to cooperate in any way. They opposed the new government because it was just as much a military regime as the previous one had been and because General Farrell remained as president. In the light of subsequent events, their policy was a badly mistaken one. Juan Alvarez, who succeeded Avalos as minister of justice a few days after the coup, tried in vain to organize a civilian ministry. If the party leaders had joined with him to organize a strong democratic government which would have promised to maintain the social reforms of the *de facto* regime, it seems more than likely that Perón would not be president of Argentina today.

Instead, the political party leaders demanded the resignation of President Farrell and the transference of executive power to the Supreme Court. This was a tactless move in view of the fact that that highest judicial body had the reputation, as do many supreme courts, of being very conservative. Many workers who might have been won over to the anti-Perón side feared that a government organized by the Supreme Court would try to abolish the social reforms which Perón had carried out.

The pig-headed behavior of many employers during this moment of crisis weakened the anti-Perón cause. The Avalos coup occurred just a few days before October 12, the Day of the Race throughout Latin America, which had been proclaimed by Perón as a legal, paid holiday. After the coup many employers immediately announced that they had no intention of paying their workers for not working on that day and that business would go on as usual. This action of course increased the workers' fears that the overthrow of Perón would result in destruction of all the gains they had made while he was secretary of labor.

The Peronistas had not been napping during these events. Riots occurred in Buenos Aires and some of the provincial cities from the first day of the Avalos upset. Several people were killed in clashes with police. As the indecision continued and the politicians and anti-Perón military men remained stalemated, unable to form a responsible government, the pro-Perón demonstrations began to take on a more organized form.

The packinghouse workers in Avellaneda, Berisso, and other cities around Buenos Aires were particularly active. Cipriano Reyes and other leaders of the new packinghouse workers unions began to lay plans for a move to seize power and put Colonel Perón and his friends back in office. By October 15 the rioting had assumed major proportions, and a move had started in the packinghouses for a general strike in support of Colonel Perón.

On the sixteenth of October the packinghouse workers began to move on Buenos Aires. That day and the next they arrived in truckloads, on trains, some even on foot. They began to take over the city. Urging the workers of the capital to join them in their support of the deposed labor secretary, the packinghouse workers were not loath to use force if persuasion was to no avail. By October 17 the city was virtually in their hands.

The Army did not lift a finger to oppose the movement. Had they wanted to, the Army could probably have suppressed the rioting and disorder, but only at the expense of many lives.

This was a toll which the Army did not want to be accused of exacting. The military elements which had thrown out Perón were not willing to fight against the Peronista mobs.

There were undoubtedly Army groups which joined the attempt to restore Perón. A year later retired Captain Ramón E. Virasoro was quoted as saying that he had worked with other military men in the period just before October 17 to organize such a movement. Captain Virasoro claimed that it was due to the efforts of General Humberto Sosa Molina that the Third Infantry Regiment stationed in the capital did not turn out to oppose the pro-Perón demonstrators.

So the Peronista mobs met no resistance. They ranged the streets in a more or less organized fashion, closing down stores and factories which would not obey the *ad hoc* general strike call. One Socialist, an ex-official of Unión Ferroviaria, tells the story of being chased from a sidewalk café by a Peronista mob. He fled to a near-by hotel and was pursued madly through its corridors. He was finally able to slip out a back entrance and get lost in the crowd. Such incidents no doubt were not uncommon.

Meanwhile, the leaders of the C.G.T. were hesitating. Although they had supported Perón for a year and a half and had been virtually his prisoners, they were not now too anxious to come to his rescue. They did not relish a clash with the military, nor were they convinced that any move by the unions could bring Colonel Perón back to power. So they procrastinated, hoping that the situation would right itself. Late on the evening of October 17, when the city was in the hands of pro-Perón mobs and the Colonel was already freed, the C.G.T. finally resolved to call a twenty-four hour nationwide general strike for the eighteenth of October in favor of Perón's return to power. Their hesitancy on this occasion did not prevent them in future years from proclaiming October 17 and the general strike of that day and the next as their own special holiday—and Juan Domingo Perón has never seen fit to challenge them on this matter.

Meanwhile, the new government was wavering. On the sixteenth General Avalos announced that Perón had never been "arrested," that he had only been "in protective custody." On the seventeenth the Colonel was brought back to Buenos Aires, taken to the Central Military Hospital and then released. A few hours later he appeared on the balcony of the Casa Rosada, in company of President Farrell. Farrell announced that Perón was free, that the executive power would not be turned over to the Supreme Court and that the Avalos government was out of office. A crowd which filled the Plaza de Mayo to overflowing wildly cheered Colonel Perón.

The denouement was a complete success for Perón. Although he did not return to any of his offices—because he almost immediately became a candidate for the presidency— he undoubtedly resumed his position as strong man of the government. His close friend and collaborator, Lieutenant Colonel Domingo Mercante, was made Secretary of Labor and Social Welfare in his place, while another close friend, Colonel Velazco, was reinstated as head of the Federal Police and a third associate, General Pistarini, took Perón's old post as vice president. The defeated General Avalos resigned his military posts on October 18 and that same day Admiral Vernengo Lima, the other half of the two-man Avalos cabinet, was arrested. He was held for a few days before being released, and he resigned from the Navy.

The events of October 17 indicated that large sections of the organized working class supported Perón, particularly those unions organized through the aid of the Secretary of Labor and Social Welfare. All attempts by the opposition to claim that the coup was carried out by force, or with the cooperation of the government, and so on, cannot efface the fact that the general strike of October 17 and 18 was virtually nation-wide and that at the time no sizable labor group dared to oppose it.

The failure of this attempt to oust Perón is in large part attributable to the anti-Peronista politicians who hesitated when it was time to act. What was needed then was the formation of a government that could take the place of the one which had fallen with Perón, and which could act decisively. It would have had the support of the most important elements of the military.

If the new government had made it clear that it did not intend to go back on any of the gains made by the workers under Perón, it could have asked for—and would very likely have received—the cooperation of the C.G.T. and other trade union bodies. If, for instance, a labor leader of some distinction had immediately been made secretary of labor, and a government consisting of Radicals, Socialists, and Progressive Democrats had been set up with the support of the Army, it seems highly unlikely that the upheaval of October 17 would have taken place.

In this instance "he who hesitates is lost" was a more appropriate sign post for the opposition than "all things come to those who wait."

"THE IMPOSSIBLE
CANDIDACY"

𒀀

EVEN AFTER the incident of October 17 most foreign observers and most of the anti-Peronistas still felt that Perón would not be successful in his bid for the presidency. The Colonel's opponents jeeringly called him "the impossible candidate," because some months earlier Perón had said that his running for president would be "impossible," that he had no presidential ambitions. However, even before the unsuccessful Avalos coup he had, in the manner of politicians, changed his mind and announced his candidacy.

The burden of the campaign was carried by the Partido Laborista, an organization established in November, 1945, by Perón's adherents among the labor leaders. Most of the important trade union figures in Argentina joined the Partido Laborista, which was headed by Luis Gay, president of the Telephone Workers Federation, and Cipriano Reyes, leader of the packinghouse workers and hero of October 17.

Locals of the Partido Laborista sprang up all over the country. The party was formally organized by some 2,000 delegates at its first convention in November, 1945. The party platform pledged it to work for nationalization of railways, telephones, electric companies; suppression of trusts; the building of hospitals, public baths, workers' houses, homes for the aged and infirm; restriction of the power of the police to make political or trade union arrests; and defense of the social gains made while Perón was secretary of labor. The Labor Party named Perón as its candidate for president and Lieutenant Colonel Domingo Mercante, Perón's successor as secretary of labor, as nominee for vice president.

At the party's chief campaign rally in Buenos Aires, Luis Gay, the president of the Partido Laborista, declared that "It is our aim that the first worker of Argentina, Colonel Perón, shall be president. . . . It is not true that the labor unions are interested only in their own interests. We want the scientific and cultural development of the Argentine nation." At the same meeting, Luis Monsalvo, an old railroad union leader and secretary of the new party, said: "Like the British Labor Party, the Argentine Labor Party maintains that it will not tolerate obstructions to the will of the Argentine people. We will never tolerate, under any circumstances, the exploitation of the people." He pledged that the Labor Party would fight against "powerful forces composed of big landowners . . . bankers and those who live on incomes."

The other wing of Peronista support came from a dissident group in the Unión Civica Radical. In 1945 three second-rate Radical leaders were brought into the cabinet of the *de facto* regime. They were Hortensio Quijano, a walrus-moustachioed, late middle-aged Radical politician who had never played a dominant role in the Radical Party, Juan Cooke, who had been a deputy but was not one of the principal figures in the U.C.R., and Dr. Armando G. Gentille, another second-rank Radical leader. These gentlemen joined the cabinet of President Farrell as Interior Minister, Foreign Minister, and Minister of Finance, respectively.

Around Quijano, Cooke, and Gentille there rallied a small number of minor leaders of the Radical Party, who formed a Junta Renovadora de la Unión Civica Radical (Radical Reconstruction Committee). After some confusion, this group was repudiated by the Radical Party, and formed its own party in a convention attended by six hundred delegates. Perón was nominated for president and Quijano for vice president.

Then and later there was an attempt on the part of many Peronistas to portray Perón as the logical and ideological successor to the old Radical leader Hipólito Irigoyen, in spite of the fact that Perón and most of his military adherents had been active in the 1930 revolution which drove Irigoyen out of office. Thus Enrique Eduardo García, a Peronista recruit from the Radical camp, in a pamphlet entitled "Radiografía Política del General Perón," wrote as follows:

Hipólito Irigoyen and Radicalism and the proletarian masses have their revenger in Juan Perón. The so-called revolution of the sixth of September 1930 was nothing more than a conspiracy of traitors, perjurers and ultra-conservatives. . . . What they did against that other Conductor, Chief and Leader was revolting to common decency . . . they moved him from jail to jail . . . they tried him and finally put him in Martín García Penitentiary. . . . They freed him, figuring that he was soon to die. He died. . . . Ah, divine vengeance has at last been found for this most cultured, most liberal, most calm of men, in the person of Perón!

García's enthusiasm leads him to ignore the fact that Perón was one of those whom he accuses of having mistreated Irigoyen. Perón himself made the same error when, in launching the campaign of his dissident Radical supporters, he claimed that there was present "The nucleus of Irigoyen Radicalism which is the purest movement Argentina has had in all its history. Our doctrine attempts to interpret and carry out the ideas of Irigoyen which are the basis of our conception of the State."

The two Peronista forces for a while presented the spectacle of having the same candidate for the post of chief executive and rival candidates for the vice presidency. It was some time before an accord was reached and Hortensio Quijano was supported for vice president by both parties.

Meanwhile, the opposition had been having a very difficult time unifying its ranks. Most of the anti-Peronista forces agreed in theory that they should band together against the Colonel's candidacy. However, the Radicals' traditional policy was opposed to coalescing with other political groups, and there was strong pressure within the party ranks not to break this tradition, in spite of the particular circumstances which now confronted the country.

The other anti-Perón groups tried to ease the way toward coalition. The Socialists agreed to support whomsoever the Radical Party nominated, if some formula for united action could be adopted. The Progressive Democratic Party, whose chief strength is in the province of Santa Fé, took the same stand, while the Conservative Party never did nominate any candidate.

The Communists were willing to cooperate with the other anti-Peronista groups, though some of these were not so anxious to cooperate with the Communists. The remaining trade union groups which were behind the coalition and the student groups which were very active in the whole anti-Perón campaign were particularly opposed to working with the Communists. However, the Communists were finally admitted to the coalition and took an active part in the election.

The Radicals were now free to nominate their own candidates for president and vice president. Their convention, meeting on December 31 in Buenos Aires, named José P. Tamborini and Enrique P. Mosca for president and vice president, respectively. The Radicals had already decided to join the Socialists, Progressive Democrats, and Communists in establishing the Unión Democrática, which was formally organized on November 15, 1945, and which from then on directed the presidential campaign of the anti-Peronista forces.

One more problem faced the opposition: whether or not to run joint slates for members of the Chamber of Deputies and the Senate. The Radicals objected very strongly to carrying the coalition policy that far, and it was finally decided to leave the individual parties free to run their own slates. In most localities, therefore, separate lists were put up by the Radicals, Socialists, and Communists, while in Santa Fé a Progressive Democratic slate was offered and in some provinces the Conservatives put up candidates. The competing slates undoubtedly weakened the anti-Perón movement.

The campaign was hectic and bitter. There was violence on both sides—though Tamborini and Mosca were on the receiving end more often than Perón and Quijano. The authorities were quite frankly in favor of Perón and did little to hide this favoritism. When the opposition leaders protested to the Minister of Interior after Peronistas had fired on a Democratic Union election rally and killed four people, the Minister turned a deaf ear to their pleas. At the funeral of the four victims other shots were fired and three more people were killed. Perón formally denounced such acts of violence; this seemed to have but little effect on his followers. He had a taste of opposition violence himself when his campaign train was derailed on returning to Buenos Aires from the interior.

The campaigns of the two groups differed fundamentally. Neither Tamborini nor Mosca, both old-line Radical politicians, had the personality to inspire audiences greatly. They toured the country widely, laying most stress on the fact that Perón was a dictator and that to vote for him was to vote for a Fascist, but they failed dismally to arouse widespread enthusiasm for their cause—an enthusiasm necessary to counteract the almost fanatical devotion of Perón's followers.

Tamborini traced his political lineage back through Hipólito Irigoyen to Demosthenes and Socrates, but neither he nor
his running mate seriously discussed the issues which Perón
had made the real ones of the campaign—social problems.
Even the Socialists and Communists skirted the social and
economic issues. As usual, coalition meant restraint—and re-
strained campaigning would not defeat Perón.

Moreover, Mosca was an unfortunate choice. He was particularly disliked in the province of Santa Fé, where he had
once acted as "interventor" for the Federal government and
had won many enemies. In addition, his name (meaning "fly"
in Spanish) was often turned against him. In Rosario this
writer saw a wall on which some Unión Democrática stalwart
had painted in large letters the words "Vote por Mosca!"
(Vote for Mosca!). A Peronista had come along and with a
few deft strokes of the paint brush had changed this to "Por
Moscas, Use Flit!" (For Flies, Use Flit!).

The whole emphasis of the opposition campaign was on the
issue of democracy. On the contrary, Perón constantly reit-
erated the two issues of social reform and Argentine nationalism. He went up and down the country telling the workers
what he had done for them as secretary of labor and pointing
to his accomplishments as an augury of what he would do
were he elected president. He called for support from trade
unions which he had helped organize and workers for whom
he had secured wage increases.

The climax of Perón's well-planned campaign was the issu-
ance of a government decree about two weeks before Christmas, 1945, ordering all employers to give their workers a
Christmas bonus equivalent to 25 percent of their total yearly
pay. The government itself was carefully exempted from this
law, but this fact was overlooked in the furor which arose as a
consequence of its proclamation. The Secretary of Labor announced it as a new "triumph" for Perón. The employers

were confounded; the workers were jubilant. At least the more unsophisticated of the latter regarded this windfall as new evidence of Perón's laborism.

The organized employers made it clear that they regarded this decree as unconstitutional and intended to ignore it. Long after Christmas many employers had still not paid the bonus. On January 10 the National Association of Department Stores declared a lockout in Buenos Aires as a protest against the decree and the following day the Assembly of Argentine Industry, Commerce and Production declared a three-day protest lockout.

There is no doubt that this decree and the reaction of the employer interests to it were important factors in rallying working-class support for Perón. Another incident helping the Peronistas was the decision of the Supreme Court early in February that the Secretariat of Labor and Social Welfare was unconstitutional. This confirmed the opinion which many workers had held of the Supreme Court at the time of the October events.

Perón cunningly played on Argentine nationalism. He and his friends made the phrase "Braden o Perón" (Braden or Perón) a campaign slogan. The Peronistas made it appear that the candidate of the opposition was not the mild-mannered Dr. Tamborini, but the late American Ambassador. "Braden o Perón" was painted on every wall and pasted on every window. In a speech before 120,000 followers in Buenos Aires, Perón accused Braden of having interfered in Argentine internal affairs and of organizing opposition to the government as part of "an oligarchical Communist alliance." He denounced Braden as the organizer and head of a spy ring covering all Latin America and as financing the campaign against Perón with money "extorted from Argentine businessmen." The Peronistas continuously reminded the people of Argentina that Perón had stood up to the Colossus of the North and had triumphed.

The Peronista paper *La Epoca* published a cartoon with two panels. In one, Hitler, standing before a map of Europe dated "The Year 1937," is saying, "Poland is a danger to the world"; in the other, Braden stands before a map of the American hemisphere dated "The Year 1946" and proclaims that "Argentina is a danger to peace."

The Peronistas' twin appeals to class and national feeling were more effective than the Unión Democrática realized—until the election was over. The opposition consistently underestimated the attraction which Perón had for the rank and file worker of Argentina. With the exception of the Communists, they mistakenly pitched their campaign on the high plane of a discussion of political philosophies. The Communists talked about democracy and fascism, too, but emphasized their arguments with earthy insults and street clashes with Peronistas.

The Peronistas insisted that their opponents stood for the "oligarchy" and that, if the opposition won, the workers of Argentina would return to the unfavorable conditions prevalent before 1943. Although the opposition staunchly declared that they would not alter the social reform measures of the *de facto* government, and that they objected only to the dictatorial aspects of that regime, these assurances were not too widely accepted. The workers noted the obvious haste of employers to throw over this social legislation and the political support they gave to the opposition.

As a result of the underestimation of Perón's influence on the laboring class, the opposition was sure right down to the day the final returns came in that they had won the election. On the day after the poll, spokesmen for all anti-Perón groups, including Tamborini, Mosca, Socialist Nicolás Repetto, Radical leader Eduardo Laurencena, Progressive Democratic leader Julio A. Noble, and Communist Rodolfo Ghioldi, issued statements declaring that the election had been the cleanest in the history of the country, and praising the Army for having kept perfect order during the poll.

Candidate Tamborini had announced before the election that "If the elections are only half-way correct, the democratic parties will win handsomely," and on the night of the balloting he said: "My impression with regard to the normality and cleanness of the election is very good. . . . In speaking of correct elections, I am speaking—with a few unimportant exceptions—of the whole country. From all of the provincial committees, furthermore, we are receiving absolute predictions of victory."

Nicolás Repetto was quoted as saying that "according to information received up until this moment these elections can be considered as correct and normal as were those first ones held under the Saenz Peña law" (when the secret ballot and other precautions were first introduced, in 1916).

The anti-Perón papers were positive that their side had won. *La Nación* in its stuffy way announced that "With Exemplary Correctness the Elections Were Held Yesterday Throughout the Nation," while *La Crítica* announced "A Smashing Democratic Triumph Expected." *El Mundo* noted that "After Many Years Buenos Aires Votes Normally," and *La Razón* said, "The Radical and Socialist Headquarters Were the Center of Extraordinary and Jubilant Activity" on election night.

There is little doubt that the actual mechanics of balloting on February 24, 1946, were run with a correctness which had not been seen in decades. Both Peronistas and their opponents testified to this. The election was in the hands of the Armed Forces who had pledged themselves to an honest vote. They had urged all citizens to go to the polls. Posters appeared in the streets during the preelection period reading, "Citizen: On the 24th of February 1946 the Armed Forces of the Nation Will Guarantee You Your Freedom to Vote" and "Vote, Fellow Citizen, under the Guarantee of the Armed Forces of the Nation—the Army, Navy and Air Force."

All sides seemed agreed that the Armed Forces acted in an unbiased way on this occasion. Tamborini in his statement on election night said: "The Army on this historic day has lived up to its responsibilities to the country. Its presence has been sufficient to assure the people clean elections."

That the balloting on February 24 was honest is certain. However, the oppositionists were correct in their statements after their defeat that they had been subject to a great deal of pressure, violence, and intimidation in the campaign period. This point was perhaps overdone in opposition statements in the months succeeding February 24, 1946. But it is a fact worthy of mention.

It remains true, however, that Perón and his supporters won a resounding popular victory on February 24, 1946. Perón was elected by the largest electoral vote in the country's history and by a substantial popular majority. At the same time the Peronistas won almost two thirds of the seats in the Chamber of Deputies and all but two in the Senate. For the first time in forty years the Socialists failed to elect even one member of the Chamber of Deputies, while the once-dominant Conservatives placed only two deputies and the Radicals were reduced to forty-four seats.

Even in the city of Buenos Aires, which had been overwhelmingly Radical and Socialist, the Peronistas came in first with about a quarter of a million votes, the Radicals were second with 150,000, and the Socialists polled third with a little over a hundred thousand. The Communists were a poor fourth.

In the provinces the Peronistas did just as well, electing

all of the provincial governors and securing majorities in all
the provincial legislatures save that of Corrientes.

Thus the Peronista Revolution was a reality. More than a
year before the election Perón had proclaimed the end of
the "military phase" of the revolution; the results of February
24 made clear its popular triumph as well. Perón himself
showed how he viewed the results of the poll in a discussion
of his ideas concerning revolutions and their legitimacy:

What happens is that occasionally, very occasionally, a revolution
is necessary, even as promoter of political and social progress, or
more modestly, as a means to put an end to indefensible situations
for which there is no other way out, either in fact or in law. But
let it be clear that a revolutionary act is not, in itself, democratic
or anti-democratic, dictatorial or anti-dictatorial. It will be one
or the other according to the intentions for which it is carried out.
Revolutions may be legitimized by the consensus of public opinion
and because they are considered as having served lofty aims or
put an end to a corrupt political situation. Regarding at least my
personal participation in the movement of June 4, 1943 it is indisputable that it has been legitimized by the popular demonstration of October 17, 1945 and by the elections, free, completely
free, of February 1946.

Perón had now achieved his ambition—to be the Constitutional President of Argentina.

THE POLITICS OF A DICTATORSHIP

৪৩৪

AFTER FEBRUARY 24, 1946, Perón would not have had to be a dictator. He was elected by a solid majority; his party controlled both houses of Congress. He could have acted like a constitutional, democratic president, but for reasons best known to himself, he did not choose to do so. As the months of his presidency became years his regime became increasingly oppressive, increasingly dictatorial. Although he had the opportunity, Juan Domingo Perón did not choose to be a democrat.

His membership in the G.O.U. is prima-facie evidence that he places no very high value on political democracy and its corollaries of free speech, free press, and freedom of association. Further indication of this is found in his speeches and writings. In a pamphlet on the "Political and Social Situation Prior to the Revolution of 1943" Perón has written that:

Possibly, it originated at least under certain of its aspects, in different vices of a universal nature which, if not inherent to the democratic *doctrine,* were inherent to the *practice* of democracy. . . . Whoever wishes to consider political questions without hypocrisy must acknowledge that all the democratic system was based upon hollow principles, because what really counted—and I have stated this on other occasions—was not the regime itself but its outward form. And what is even more serious, democracy

54 POLITICS OF A DICTATORSHIP

was used by the powerful classes as a factor of coercion against the humble. All the system was based on the equality of individual rights; but as economic situations were very different, such an equality of rights was merely a form of words.

Socialists and other social reformers the world over have agreed with Perón's condemnation of the wedding of political democracy and social and economic exploitation, but most have also come to the conclusion that there is no guarantee of an end to economic and social exploitation if political democracy is sacrificed, and indeed that the end of such exploitation is virtually impossible once political democracy has been destroyed. This is an opinion which Juan Domingo Perón apparently does not share.

CIPRIANO REYES AND OTHER DISSIDENT PERONISTAS

Political crises have popped like firecrackers during the Perón administration. The opposition, though increasingly muzzled, has occasionally shown a certain nuisance value. But it is among Perón's own followers that he has had the greatest difficulty. His was a political movement which developed very rapidly and included people of varied political, social, and economic points of view. Among his adherents were more than the ordinary number of opportunists and place-seekers. Among them, too, were a number of idealists—and these have probably given Perón more trouble than his more venal subordinates.

The first crisis within the ranks of Peronismo after February 24 came when General Perón decided to unify his followers in one political organization. Right after his election, he began steps to bring together the Partido Laborista, the pro-Perón Radicals, and the Independents who had supported his candidacy. As early as March, 1946, he spoke of the possibility of forming a Partido Unico de la Revolución (Single Party of the Revolution).

However, this plan aroused a great deal of dissension

among his supporters, particularly among the Laboristas. This group had of course arisen from the trade unions, the first civilian group to rally around Perón. Many—if not most —of the leaders of the Partido Laborista looked upon their party as a real labor party, not merely a Peronista party. They regarded Peronismo as an opportunity to gain for the trade union movement and for the workers the things which they had failed to achieve during long years of governmental neglect. These leaders hoped to form around Perón a political organization—the Partido Laborista—which in future times could fight strongly for the rights and wishes of the workers whether or not Perón was still in power.

These leaders took a very dim view of their chief's proposal that they amalgamate with the pro-Perón Radicals and other groups which had supported "El Líder" in the February elections. The dissident Radicals included a sizable number of second- or third-rate politicians who had not had much opportunity to get ahead in the Unión Civica Radical and who had seized upon the Peronista movement as a chance to better their fortunes. These people, for the most part opportunists, had little if anything in common with the program of the Partido Laborista. The only thing which united them with the Laboristas was the fact that both groups backed General Perón.

Chief of the Laborista opposition to Peronista unity was Cipriano Reyes, leader of the packinghouse workers and key figure in the events of October 17. Reyes was a small, nervous man, who had catapulted to fame and position as a result of his organizational activities among the packinghouse workers. He had been successively a Socialist, an anarchist, and a Peronista, and he had a reputation as being a man who would not shrink at using violence if it would gain him his ends.

Next to Perón, Reyes was probably the most controversial man in Argentina in 1946. His friends nearly worshiped him, feeling that he was the spokesman for all the country's depressed workers, that he was a man of intense bravery and of true devotion to the cause of labor. His enemies, on the other hand, maintained that he was a gangster who had taken advantage of the Perón Revolution to get to the top and that he was seeking to out-Perón Perón in demagoguery and violence.

This writer, who spoke to Reyes several times late in 1946 and who was particularly interested in finding out as much about him as possible, felt that he was a man of sincerity, a courageous man who had taken upon himself the dangerous work of organizing labor in a traditionally anti-union industry. In his job he had to meet force with force. Reyes's desire for social reform and for improving the condition of the workers was undoubtedly not unmixed with ambition, but, had he been interested only in attaining power and prestige, he would have stuck with Perón, who was then at the height of his influence. On the other hand, Reyes was a man of little formal education and showed a certain political naïveté in the timing of his break with Perón.

When Perón in March, 1946, first proposed liquidating the Partido Laborista, Reyes and other labor leaders violently objected. The President immediately dropped the suggestion, but soon after his inauguration announced in a radio speech that the Partido Laborista, the pro-Perón Radical party, and the Independents were to be merged into the Partido Unico.

This news took the labor leaders by surprise, and the parliamentarians of the Partido Laborista immediately met. They had a majority in both the Senate and the Chamber and if they had desired to hold out against Perón, might conceivably have had their way. At first, under Reyes's lead, they almost unanimously announced their opposition to the scheme.

The government quickly applied pressure to the Laborista

deputies and senators. Just what this pressure consisted of, probably only the congressmen could tell with accuracy. In any case, the one-time united front of the Laboristas in opposition to the Partido Unico began to melt away. Attendance at successive meetings of the Laborista congressional bloc gradually dwindled until, finally, no more than two dozen remained.

Meanwhile, Reyes, who was vice president of the Partido Laborista, called together the party's executive and it summoned a party convention. This meeting was attended by delegates from all over the country—virtually the same people who had organized the party a year earlier. It was resolved that the Partido Laborista should continue in existence regardless of the decisions of its congressional representatives.

However, in spite of apparently widespread support on the part of the members of the Partido Laborista, fewer and fewer of its leaders dared take a stand against the Partido Unico. Among the defectionists was Luis Gay, the party's president, head of the Telephone Workers Federation, and one of the two or three most active Peronistas among the trade union leaders. He believed in the Partido Laborista as a real working-class movement which would seek to carry out the wishes of the workers, and he did not look with favor upon its dissolution. However, he did not feel that the time was ripe to break with Perón. He felt that there was still more to be gained by going along with Perón, and working within the united Peronista party. He therefore refused to join Reyes in maintaining the Partido Laborista.

Reyes became increasingly bitter in his attacks on Perón. He accused Perón of betraying the movement which had put him in power, of selling out to the very elements of the plutocracy against which he had inveighed so loudly. At the same time, in a little book entitled *Qué es el Laborismo?* ("What Is

Laborism?"), Reyes put down his own philosophy of what the Laborista movement was supposed to be. He also tried vainly to keep in line the dwindling ranks of his supporters. Only one other deputy, Dr. Bericke, and three or four members of the Buenos Aires provincial legislature stayed with Reyes.

The tide was running too strongly in favor of Perón for Cipriano Reyes to buck it. His only active support came from among the packinghouse workers in the environs of Buenos Aires. Although other workers may have sympathized with his point of view and trusted his motives, they would not follow him in opposition to Perón. Increasingly isolated politically, he became the victim of growing persecution at the hands of the government and its allies. From the middle of 1946 Reyes was subjected to half a dozen or more assassination attempts. He was booed and hissed when he attempted to speak in the Chamber of Deputies. On the other hand, the opposition did little to encourage or aid him, and by the middle of 1947 the Reyes challenge to Perón's leadership had lost most of its potency.

The Partido Laborista continued as an organization, under Reyes leadership, but all the legislators except Reyes himself deserted the party and returned to the Perón fold. When the congressional elections of March, 1948, approached, the government withdrew legal recognition from the Partido Laborista, making it impossible for the group to participate in that poll.

In mid-1948, the government sought to liquidate Reyes permanently. At that time, the Perón government announced that a vast plot to assassinate Perón and his wife had been discovered, in which Reyes and other leaders of the Partido Laborista had been involved in conjunction with John Griffiths. For several years Griffiths had been Cultural Attaché of the American Embassy. He was dismissed when the militant anti-Peronism of Spruille Braden was succeeded by the appeasement policy of George Messersmith in 1946, and had subsequently gone to Montevideo, where he had been engaging in business.

Reyes, Walter Beveraggi, the party's vice president, and other leaders of the Laboristas were jailed and held without trial for seven months. Beveraggi, who later escaped from Argentina and presented an official protest against the Perón government's behavior to the United Nations, described at length the tortures to which he, Reyes, and others had been subjected in a futile attempt to make them confess to this alleged plot. In spite of the fact that the Criminal Appeals Court announced a few months later that Reyes had *not* been tortured, wide credence was given to Beveraggi's report, which was corroborated by others.*

Griffiths, who was in Montevideo, of course denied all knowledge of or participation in any plot. Unfortunately, the American Embassy did little to try to vindicate its one-time employee, who had had the reputation of being one of the finest men ever to work in the United States Embassy in Buenos Aires.

Reyes and his friends were finally released, only to be rearrested in a few days. As these pages are being written, Reyes is still in jail—and has never been brought to trial. Beveraggi escaped to Uruguay and then came to the United

* Nowhere is the totalitarianism of the Perón regime more evident than in the behavior of the Nazi-advised Federal Police. They use torture regularly to try to force confessions from their victims, and there is some indication that they have experimented with narco-hypnosis to force prisoners to confess deeds they have never committed. One case of this nature was discussed in *La Nación* of July 6, 1949:

"In the Delta a recently hidden corpse was discovered by the police, and it was supposed to be the body of a young man who had disappeared from his usual haunts. The police arrested two suspects, who finally admitted their guilt, giving minute details which were enumerated in the police report. Soon afterwards, the supposed victim turned up very much alive in Montevideo, proving that the police had been wrong. How can the confessions be explained? It's the same old story. They confessed because of fatigue, because they were worn down by beatings and terror."

States. The organization of the Partido Laborista was virtually liquidated, although Reyes did his best to direct its affairs from behind prison walls.

The Partido Unico de la Revolución was therefore formed, according to Perón's wishes. Within a few months the name Partido Unico was dropped, because it was pointed out that this had implications of following in the footsteps of Hitler and Mussolini, and Perón—who was seeking to rehabilitate himself in American eyes at that time—saw the point. After searching for an appropriate name, the denomination Partido Peronista was finally resorted to, in spite of the fact that Perón denied "personalist" ambitions.

In many cases this unification was more in name than in fact. During the next few years there were continuous interparty squabbles in the provincial organizations of the Partido Peronista. Occasionally, Perón found it necessary to send "interventors" to some locality or province to supersede the local leadership and reorganize the party's ranks. Silverio Pontieri, an early Peronista labor leader, was sent on such a mission as early as October, 1946, before the Partido Peronista was fully organized.

Numerous dissensions appeared within the Peronista ranks. In Mendoza, seven of the eighteen members of the bloc in the provincial legislature seceded to form the 24th of February Bloc, proclaiming their loyalty to Perón and his wife and accusing the local government of working with anti-Peronistas. In Bahía Blanca, in Buenos Aires province, the Peronista councilors demanded and received the resignation of the Peronista mayor. In Entre Ríos, when the Peronista bloc in the provincial senate could not agree on the list of presiding officers, the bloc split and presented two tickets.

In August, 1949, at a national convention of the Peronista Party in Buenos Aires, President Perón announced his intention to purge the membership and leadership of the party. He had already found it necessary in February, 1949, to oust the Peronista governor of Santa Fe province and replace him with a Federal interventor, Colonel Dalmiro Adaro. In elections in May, another Peronista governor, Juan Caesar, was elected, though with a majority 25,000 less than that by which the party carried the province in the Constitutional Convention elections.

These internal feuds in the Partido Peronista undoubtedly weakened the balloting strength of the party in provincial elections during 1949 and 1950. However, the Peronistas won a two-thirds majority in the Lower House of Congress and kept their unchallenged position in the Senate in the March, 1948, elections, and won once again in the special election in December, 1948, for a Constitutional Convention. The party thus held its position amazingly well for a group that had been in office for four years. In part this continued popular support was due to the growing suppression of the opposition, making it increasingly hard for the anti-Peronistas to get their side of the picture across to the public. The opposition was largely ineffective.

In the election of February, 1946, the Radical Party was the chief opposition group, winning forty-four seats in the Chamber of Deputies and two in the Senate, while the Conservative or National Democratic Party gained two seats in the Chamber and the Progressive Democrats one. These parties constituted the opposition in Congress. Soon they were joined by Cipriano Reyes and Dr. Bericke, who, though continuing to sit on the Peronista side of the House, in fact were united with the opposition on most issues.

The Peronista government showed its attitude toward the opposition very early when it refused to seat the two anti-Peronista senators elected from the province of Corrientes in the 1946 poll. On the pretext that there had been fraud in the elections in the province, the Senate refused to accept their credentials and promised an investigation of the circumstances surrounding their election. The two Radical senators were never seated. Their seats were filled by two Peronistas in elections finally held in 1949.

The Supreme Court of the nation was dealt with even more cavalierly than the opposition members of the Senate. Late in 1946 Perón announced his intention of impeaching the whole Supreme Court. One judge, Roberto Repetto, resigned; the rest resisted the attempt of the government to oust them. The cynicism of the regime is clearly shown by the fact that the Court was impeached on the grounds that it had ruled as legitimate the acts of the *de facto* government of 1943–45. The whole Court was finally ousted and judges more sympathetic to Perón were installed. The lower courts were also purged.

However, the real muzzling of the opposition did not come in the legislative halls or in the courtrooms. For the most part the Radicals were able to speak quite freely from their seats in the Chamber of Deputies until 1949. It was something else again when it came to the *publication* of these speeches or anything else which was contrary to the Peronista government.

GAGGING THE PRESS

In preparation for the 1946 election, the *de facto* government lifted the restrictions on freedom of the press, and in the election campaign most of the papers were anti-Peronista. The two deans of Argentine journalism, *La Prensa* and *La Nación,* throughout the *de facto* regime and on into the Perón administration continued to attack the government. Their disapproval was usually couched in rather dignified and ponderous terms, but it was unfavorable criticism, nevertheless.

Among other major dailies more or less critical of the administration were *La Razón* and *La Critica.* The latter journal had carried on the most active fight against Nazi and Fascist influence in Argentina during the Castillo administration, and it spoke up frequently for democracy in the succeeding years. *La Razón* also criticized the government with some acerbity.

Various weekly sheets were a great deal more acid in their comments on the regime than the dailies allowed themselves to be. The leader of this group was *La Vanguardia,* the organ of the Socialist Party, which in bitter cartoons, in satirical articles, and in more weighty pieces by the party's Grand Old Men Repetto, Dickman, and Palacios, parried with and hammered at the government. In addition there were *Provincias Unidas,* the organ of the Radical Party, and *Argentina Libre,* a paper founded by exiles in Montevideo but moved to Buenos Aires in the middle of 1946.

These papers had large circulations and were avidly read by the opponents of the administration. In the first few months after Perón's inauguration, they experienced little difficulty, except that from time to time numbers would not be delivered to subscribers and dealers in the provinces, or newsboys selling the papers would be assaulted in Buenos Aires.

It was not until 1947 that the government began seriously to move against the opposition press. The first attack was made on the weeklies. Various pretexts were used for closing them down. Typical was the case of *La Vanguardia,* which was closed after a municipal inspector visited its presses in the cellar under the Socialist Party headquarters, found that the place was "too dirty and unhealthy," pointed out a number of minor violations of city health regulations, and ordered the cessation of all printing in the *La Vanguardia* shop. Wherever the editors attempted to print the paper the same conditions were suddenly "discovered."

The proprietors of *La Vanguardia* immediately corrected

the specific conditions against which the health inspector had complained and asked for a new investigation. However, a year and a half passed before another inspector was sent to look over the premises. This time Police Inspector Armando Otamendi sent in a favorable report, urging that printing be allowed to go forward. However, within forty-eight hours Otamendi was fired from his job and the paper was still not allowed to appear.

The same kind of indirection was used in attacking the larger and more widely circulated daily papers. Important Peronista officials "bought into" several papers, including *La Razón* and *La Critica*. Sra. Perón herself bought *Noticias Gráficas,* which had at one time bitterly opposed her husband. The story is told of Sra. Perón's meeting the proprietor of this paper and telling him that she had heard that he had received offers to buy. When he hesitatingly replied in the affirmative, she asked how much he would need to receive in order to make the sale worth while. Upon his naming six million pesos as the amount, she is reported to have answered, "As of right now, *Noticias Gráficas* is mine."

As *La Nación* and *La Prensa* held out against all attempts at bribery or intimidation, the government began to bring economic pressure on these two great dailies. At first this was done through their newsprint supplies. Most newsprint used in Argentina is imported, and these two dailies had brought in large stocks of paper. Suddenly in 1947 the government stopped granting foreign exchange for the importation of newsprint. Using the scarcity of dollars as a pretext, the government decreed that from then on licenses to import newsprint would be granted more sparingly, and that those papers with "excess" supplies would have to give them up. Under this "legal" sanction, the government seized thousands of tons of newsprint from *La Prensa* and *La Nación,* turning most of it over to pro-Peronista papers.

Next the government made it impossible for *La Prensa* and *La Nación* to import their own paper so that, when their reserve supplies were exhausted, these two dailies became dependent on the government for their newsprint. Publication was on a day-to-day basis, and several times they announced that unless the government provided them with more paper they would have to close down within a few days. The government, for its part, doled out the paper in small enough amounts to keep the two opposition dailies always on edge as to whether or not they could publish.

La Prensa and *La Nación* naturally received no government subsidies such as undoubtedly are used to keep some of the Peronista papers alive. They therefore depended on advertising for most of their revenue. So, as the second step in its attack, the Argentine government decreed a limitation on the size of newspapers to sixteen pages, and provided that only a small portion of each issue could consist of advertising copy. Since *La Prensa* and *La Nación* had often run to several score pages, the largest part of which was advertising, the decree was calculated to hit them where it hurt most. They were virtually the only papers printing more than sixteen pages.

Meanwhile, the provincial anti-Peronista press was effectively closed down by congressional action. As a result of the allegations of Walter Beveraggi concerning the torturing of himself, Cipriano Reyes, and others, the opposition members of the Chamber of Deputies demanded an inquiry into the methods being used by the police. They proposed that Congress set up an investigating committee. In the face of considerable public pressure, the Peronista bloc in Congress finally accepted the suggestion, but appended to it the proposal that the committee also investigate charges by the Peronista press that the anti-Perón newspapers had been subsidized by the opposition political parties during the 1946 campaign, and that some had also been subsidized from abroad, particularly from the United States.

A committee was appointed, headed by deputies J. A. Visca and Rudolph Decker. The body devoted all of its attention to investigating the Peronista charges against the opposition and paid no attention to the allegations of torture which had originally brought it into existence. The committee took upon itself vast powers. It subpoenaed the books of the chief opposition newspapers, including *La Prensa* and *La Nación*, and ordered police stationed in the business offices of the two papers. It began a campaign of closing papers which were not in accord with the regime. Most of these newspapers were shut on the grounds that they had insulted the national honor by not putting at their masthead "Year of the Liberator San Martín" starting with the January 1, 1950, issues, as provided in a decree published during the closing days of 1949.

Some sixty-five papers were closed by the Visca Committee between Christmas Day, 1949, and January 29, 1950. These included the country's leading Catholic paper, *El Pueblo,* which was later allowed to reopen; another Catholic paper, *Los Principios* of the province of Córdoba; one of the oldest Argentine papers, *El Intransigente* of Salta, *Clarín* of Buenos Aires, and many others. Many of the papers were closed permanently. When Peronista Deputy Ricardo Salamon from Salta asked that *El Intransigente* be allowed to reopen, the Peronista bloc in Congress expelled him.

Finally, early in 1951, the Perón administration moved to close down *La Prensa* completely. The occasion for this move was the government's smashing of a strike of Unión Ferroviaria late in January, 1951, and the necessity of turning the attention of the workers from this anti-labor action to a situation in which the Perón government could once again be pictured as the workers' Saint George killing the capitalist dragon.

The vehicle used to close down the paper was the Buenos Aires newsboys' union, a Peronista group which the government had organized in 1946 to break the anarchosyndicalist union to which the city's newsboys had long belonged. Right after the Unión Ferroviaria strike the newsboys' union presented a long list of demands and insisted that they be accepted *in toto* or the newsdealers would refuse to handle *La Prensa*. The real motive of the demands was demonstrated by their extreme nature. Included were provisions that 20 percent of the paper's revenue from classified ads be turned over to the union, that offices which the paper maintained throughout Buenos Aires to receive classified ads be shut down, and that large pay increases and other benefits be granted.

The paper announced that it was willing to negotiate about these demands, but would not accept them all. However, the union demanded all or nothing, and declared a "strike" against the paper. The Peronista printing trades union then called out the paper's mechanical staff—most of whom refused to leave their jobs. Nevertheless, the paper closed down. When it attempted to open a month later, under police promises that its workers would be protected from violence, the returning workers were assaulted by Peronista gangsters and one of them was killed.

Meanwhile, the C.G.T. worked up frantic "protest meetings" and other evidences of "popular" resentment against *La Prensa*. The head of the newsvenders' union threatened that *La Nación* would soon get the same treatment as *La Prensa* if it did not report the situation more "fairly," and sycophant Peronistas demanded that the government take over the paper "in the interests of the nation." Such a move was finally undertaken by the Congressional Investigating Committee, which previously had closed down most of the rest of the country's anti-Peronista papers. Leveling charges that *La Prensa* was "subsidized" by foreigners and that its finances had been mishandled, the Committee "intervened" in the paper. Several weeks later Congress obediently passed a law nationalizing *La Prensa,* and there remained but one free paper in the country, *La Nación.* How long it could survive was anybody's guess.

"DISRESPECT"

Late in 1949 the Perón administration forged three other powerful legislative weapons against their opponents: a greatly reinforced version of an old law making it a crime to be guilty of "disrespect" of any government official; a new law for the registration of political parties; and a statute providing for the granting of dictatorial powers to the President in case of "national emergency."

For many years there had been on the books a relatively mild law punishing "disrespect" of high government officials. However, the new statute provided that proof of the correctness of a statement which was deemed "disrespectful" would be no defense against the charge of having committed a criminal act. The Chamber of Deputies had already begun to act harshly toward those of its members who were guilty of "disrespect," even before it got around to passing the new law in October, 1949. The previous June the Chamber expelled from its membership one of the leading Radicals, Deputy Rodriguez Araya, on the grounds that he had insulted President and Sra. Perón.

In December, 1949, two other Radical deputies, Atilio Cattaneo and Ernesto Sammartino, were ousted from the Chamber on charges based on the new law. In January, 1950, the Radical candidate for governor of the province of Tucumán, I. Nogués, was jailed on charges of having insulted President Perón, and so had to campaign from a jail cell. Two months later, Ricardo Balbín, Radical candidate for governor of the province of Buenos Aires, was arrested on the same charge on the day of the election. Several newspapers, including the Socialists' *Lucha,* the legal successor to *La Vanguardia,* were suppressed under provisions of the new law. The editor and assistant editor of *Lucha* were jailed for a short time.

Another law designed to tighten the noose around the neck of the opposition was passed in September, 1949. Among other things this law provided that all new political parties must wait three years before they could begin to function—to give the Federal courts time to pass on their applications for legal recognition. Parties now in existence may be dissolved if it is found that their "ideological principles" endanger "social peace," or if they have international affiliations. The law prohibits anyone who is currently registered with a political party to change his registration until after the 1952 election.

The new law also provides that each party must have a recognized provincial committee in each of the country's fourteen provinces. It prohibits any coalitions.

In part, this statute was undoubtedly aimed at dissidents in the Peronista ranks, who might conceivably seek to form other parties. In part, too, it is intended to prevent the opposition parties from uniting against the administration at any time in the future as they did in 1946. Perhaps this latter move was unnecessary since the opposition parties went their own ways in the polls held after the February, 1946, election. Another result of this new law may be to make illegal the Socialist and Progressive Democratic parties which have their strength concentrated in one or a few provinces. These parties may be unable to establish provincial organizations in every province.

The third law was passed in August, 1948. It supplemented the constitutional power to suspend constitutional guarantees under a "state of siege," by providing that the president may in case of "national emergency" assume virtually dictatorial powers over the nation's economy and political life, including the drafting of citizens for compulsory labor service under military discipline when and where he deems this necessary. The opposition argued that this law would be very useful to the government in coercing anti-Peronistas and in breaking strikes of which the government did not approve, a prediction which was borne out a year and a half later when Perón used it to break a walkout of Unión Ferroviaria.

THE OPPOSITION

The largest element of the opposition has remained the Unión Civica Radical. The Radicals were the majority party before 1943, and they have kept their position as the largest minority group and the potential majority since 1946. Convinced that the party was defeated in 1946 because it did not make a sufficient appeal to the workers, some of the younger leaders of the party have tried to out-Perón Perón. They have frequently attacked the administration as having betrayed the workers. At the time of the packinghouse workers' strike late in 1946 it was Radical Deputy Frondizzi who joined Cipriano Reyes as a chief spokesman for the strikers.

The Radical Party participated in all the elections held after 1946. In the 1948 congressional election it failed to place enough members in the Chamber of Deputies to prevent the Peronistas from getting the two thirds vote necessary to launch a move for constitutional reform. They took part in the Constitutional Convention elections late in 1948, and won virtually all the opposition seats in that body. They took part in various provincial elections and made some inroads on the Peronista strength in the provinces.

Attempts on the part of the Peronistas to split the Radical ranks were for the most part ineffective, though one or two Radical deputies did go over to Perón in the years after his election as president.

The second most important element in the opposition was the Socialist Party. Since the early 1940's its composition had considerably altered. The Peronista movement took away most of its rank and file labor support, and by the late 1940's the Socialist Party made its appeal mainly to the middle classes. It became the party of the intelligentsia par excellence, as was shown by the high intellectual caliber of its publications and the type of leadership and membership which it presented. The party had particular strength among the anti-Peronista student groups. Its publications have been among the widest read, most sprightly and most biting of those opposed to the regime.

The Socialists made some steps toward recouping their reduced fortunes in the 1948 elections when they came within a few thousand votes of replacing the Radicals as the minority among the deputies from the city of Buenos Aires, and succeeded in electing one member of the Buenos Aires provincial legislature and various members of city and town councils in that province.

The Socialists did not take part in the elections for the Constitutional Convention, proclaiming that they were opposed to amending the constitution in the manner which Perón proposed, and that the elections were merely a means of rubber-stamping Perón's determination to be reelected in 1952. They did participate in a number of provincial elections, though without any notable success, except in Buenos Aires province where they elected one provincial deputy.

The Socialists were particularly active in the trade union field, where they continued to be the driving force of the small Independent Committee of Trade Union Action (C.O.A.S.I.). However, they apparently did not have a great deal of success in attempts to make inroads into the Peronista unions.

The Communists took an equivocal position toward the Perón administration. They had violently opposed Perón's election, making copious use of the word "Peronazi" to describe his followers, and frequently clashing with them in physical encounters in the streets.

Early in 1946 the Communists abruptly began to make distinctions between "good" Peronistas and "bad" Peronistas. This change occurred shortly after the arrival in Argentina of a Soviet trade mission in March. The small Communist-controlled packinghouse workers union backed a strike called by the dominant Peronista-run union and called for general labor unity behind the walkout. Then, two days after his inauguration and on June 4, 1946, Perón announced the re-establishment of diplomatic relations with Russia. Two days later the Communist daily *La Hora* proclaimed in an editorial that the Peronista triumph on February 24, 1946, "was the result of popular unity against imperialism and the oligarchy." And in a speech to a Communist Party congress in August, Víctor Codovilla, the party's principal leader, said, "We shall support the Perón government with reservations."

In the trade unions the Communists made a sudden about-face, abandoned their rivalry to the C.G.T. and other Peronista unions, and liquidated the unions under their control. The Communist press began to compliment President Perón on his opposition to "Yankee imperialism."

When asked about this change of line, Communist leader Víctor Codovilla denied that it had anything to do with the attitude of the Peronista regime toward the Soviet Union. Rather he said the situation had changed as a result of Perón's election. The Communists had violently opposed Perón, Codovilla said, because they were sure that he was going to lose. Now they supported him because he had won, and, "after all the workers are with Perón, and if we are going to try to influence the workers, we'll have to go where they are, and gain their confidence."

However, the Socialist paper *La Vanguardia* had a different explanation when it wrote in October, 1948: "All is explained. The meridian, the axis upon which the Communists' swing, is the renewal of Argentine-Russian relations." And President Perón himself was not unaware of the meaning of the Communists' change in line. He said that "that party . . . has adopted a more skillful tactic, although a quite obvious one of infiltrating the ranks of labor. It acts as a wolf in sheep's clothing."

Whatever the motives for this about-face, it was a complete one. And it is noteworthy that for three years after the election of Perón, the Communist press was virtually untouched by the government. Although the Socialist and Radical papers were driven underground, although the meetings of both parties were interfered with and some of their leaders were forced into exile, nothing whatever happened to the Communists. Perón was using them, as they thought they were using him.

Of course, Perón gave no open evidence of supporting the Communists, but he did show them a surprisingly large degree of toleration. It is true, however, that from time to time he gave them a warning. For instance, early in 1947 the police raided a meeting of the Argentine Communist leaders, at which there were present two Chilean Communist deputies, as well as representatives of Communist parties in other neighboring countries. This raid was perhaps intended to let the Communists of Argentina know that they were being watched, and let the governments of neighboring countries know just where the leading figures of their own Communist parties were engaging in "consultation."

On their part, the Communists went out of their way to be friendly toward the Perón administration. When, in a speech in February, 1947, Perón attacked the Communists as a national menace, they did not even reply. They explained the expulsion of Radical Deputy Sanmartino from

Congress as the work of Yankee imperialists, taking no note that it was done by the Peronistas. A *La Hora* editorial referred to one of Perón's speeches as "historic," while another said that "There cannot be conflict between Peronistas and Communists in the factories."

The honeymoon of the Communists and Perón began to wane in 1949. During that year *La Hora* fell victim to the purge of the non-Peronista press. Its successor, *Pueblo Unido* was also closed by the police. Meanwhile, in several provinces local election officials refused to allow the Communists to register as a legal party, and in the province of Santiago del Estero a Communist member of the provincial legislature was not allowed to take his seat.

PERON AS A FOUNDING FATHER—THE PERONISTA CONSTITUTION

ళ❧

THE PERONISTAS' OVERWHELMING VICTORY in the congressional elections of 1948 gave Perón carte blanche to realize one of his fondest ambitions—to revise the Argentine Constitution. To do this it was necessary that Congress by a vote of two thirds of its members declare the necessity of amendment, and then that a Constitutional Convention be called to do the actual redrafting. The March, 1948, elections gave the Peronistas their necessary majority in the Chamber of Deputies; they already controlled all but two seats in the Senate. Among the first acts of the new Congress, therefore, was the declaration of the need for a revision of the Constitution. Elections for a Constitutional Convention were duly held in December.

The opposition parties were in a quandary as to whether or not they should participate in the elections. It was obvious that the Peronistas desired to revise the Constitution so that Perón would be eligible for reelection. Many opposition leaders felt that their parties' participation in the elections (which they could not win) would appear as an endorsement of this idea.

Finally after much controversy the Radicals decided to

enter candidates in the December, 1948, elections, and the Socialist Party did not. The Radicals therefore formed the opposition in the Convention. Throughout its sessions they were helpless in the face of the steam-rolling tactics of the Peronista majority. In futile protest, the Radical members of the Convention walked out several times, complaining that the opposition was being throttled, and refused to give any final assent to the new document. However, after some hesitation, Radical members of the Chamber of Deputies finally agreed to swear loyalty to it as provided in the document itself.

The work of the Constitutional Convention was more in the nature of revising the old document than of writing a new one, and the framework and much of the original wording of the 1853 document were maintained. The changes made by the Peronistas fall into six general categories: items intended to bring the Constitution up-to-date; certain structural changes in the government; measures strengthening the position of the Executive; sections injecting broad principles of social legislation; items extending the scope of permissible government economic activity; and additions making the Constitution more nationalistic.

When the Constitution of 1853 was written Argentina was little more than a collection of small warring states; the era of the railroad and airplane were unforeseen. Hence many of the changes made in 1949 reflected technological changes, and the growing tendency away from the federal form of government.

Several articles were altered to give the national government control over interprovincial traffic by railways and aircraft as well as the older forms of transportation. The increase in the country's population is indicated by the provision that deputies are to represent constituencies of at least 100,000 people. An article in the old document referring to provincial currencies in circulation in 1853 is omitted, as is a proviso concerning provincial militias. Congress is no longer enjoined "to maintain peaceful relations with the Indians, and to promote their conversion to Christianity." Finally, references to the system of trial by jury, which the authors of the 1853 document apparently hoped soon to introduce in Argentina, are omitted.

Structural changes in the form of government include abolition of indirect election of senators and the president; change of the terms of office of senators and deputies (reducing the former, increasing the latter); ending the constitutional limitation on the number of ministries. Article 44 of the old Constitution, which provided that all bills concerning taxes and the recruiting of troops originate in the Lower House, is removed.

Although some of these changes are of importance, they do not reflect any particularly Peronista influence. In a different category are those measures which serve to enhance the power of the executive. It was these alterations which were most bitterly denounced by the opposition. The president was made reeligible, thus altering the old provision that a president could be reelected "only after a similar intervening period." When questioned by the legislative chambers, the executive no longer needs to send a minister to explain its behavior, but may now choose to answer in writing. A budget no longer has to be submitted to Congress each year, but rather can be drawn up to cover as long as three years.

The power vested in Congress by the 1853 Constitution "to coin money, to regulate its value and that of foreign currency" is transferred to the president who, according to the 1949 document, "causes currency to be stamped, determines its value and that of foreign currencies."

Under the new constitution the president can veto *part* of a bill submitted to him by Congress, rather than having to accept or reject the whole measure. He now has twenty days to consider a measure rather than ten, before it becomes law. Congress no longer has power "to conduct a scrutiny" of election returns for president and vice president of the republic, "and make corrections therein," as provided in the old constitution.

Congress's power is still further restricted in favor of the executive by a provision that when extra sessions of Congress are called by the president, the legislature can only deal with "the subjects listed in the convocation."

Several features of the new constitution are designed to weaken the position of the civil power vis-à-vis the military. Article 29 of the 1949 document adds a proviso which submits civilians to court martial jurisdiction in some cases. It reads:

Members of the military forces, and persons attached thereto, are subject to military jurisdiction in the cases established by law. The same jurisdiction shall be applicable to persons who commit offenses punishable under the Code of Military Justice and are subject by law to the military tribunals.

Article 34 facilitates the declaration of martial law. The 1853 Constitution had provided for a "state of siege," which, however, could only be applied "in case of internal commotion or foreign attack endangering the exercise of this Constitution and of the authorities created by it." The new document keeps this, and appends to it another provision, as follows:

Likewise a state of precaution and alarm may be declared in the event of a disturbance of public order threatening to disrupt the normal course of life of the essential activities of the population. A law shall establish the juridical effects of such a measure, but it shall not suspend but only temporarily limit the constitutional guarantees to the extent that is indispensable. With regard to persons the powers of the President shall be reduced to detaining them or moving them from one part of the territory to another for a period not exceeding thirty days.

This new form of martial law caused one of the most violent fights in the Constitutional Convention. The opponents of the administration saw in it a handy weapon to browbeat the anti-Peronistas. They argued that the old constitution provided for a state of siege in the only two circumstances which could possibly justify the suspension of constitutional guarantees—foreign invasion or internal rebellion—and that any extension of the power of the executive to suspend the constitution was uncalled for.

Another distinctly Peronista influence in the new constitution is the social legislation sketched in it. Chapter Three of the First Division lists "Rights of the Worker, of the Family, of the Aged, and the Right to Education and Culture," while Chapter Four deals with "The Social Function of Property, Capital and Economic Activity."

"The Rights of the Worker" were enunciated by Perón in his October 17th anniversary speech in 1947, and "The Rights of the Aged" were spoken of by the president's wife during a flight of oratory sometime later. They were incorporated *in toto* into the constitution. The workers' rights according to the Peronista Constitution include the following:

1) The Right to Work
2) The Right to a Fair Reward
3) The Right to Acquire Skill
4) The Right to Worthy Working Conditions
5) The Right to Preservation of Health
6) The Right to Well-being
7) The Right to Social Security
8) The Right to the Protection of the Family
9) The Right to Economic Improvement
10) The Right to the Defense of Occupational Interests

Each of these propositions is elaborated. Oppositionists

were quick to point out that in the discussion of No. 10 there is no mention of the right of the workers to strike. This proposal is elaborated as follows:

The right freely to form trades unions and to participate in other legitimate activities designed to defend the interests of the trades constitute essential attributions of the workers, which society should respect and protect, ensuring the free exercise thereof and suppressing all acts which may prevent or impede it.

The old people's rights, as reflected by the Argentine Constitution of 1949, are the following:
1) The Right to Assistance
2) The Right to Lodging
3) The Right to Sustenance
4) The Right to Clothing
5) The Right to the Care of Physical Health
6) The Right to the Care of Moral Health
7) The Right to Recreation
8) The Right to Work
9) The Right to Tranquillity
10) The Right to Respect

In other parts of this section of the Peronista Constitution the state is pledged to support marriage and family property and to give "attention and assistance" to mothers, while it is declared that "childhood shall enjoy the special and privileged consideration of the State." Under "The Right to Education and Culture," the state is committed to provide both primary and advanced education, including university training to those who want it. A sour note in this pretty picture is the provision that:

The universities shall establish obligatory and ordinary courses designed for the students of all the faculties for their political formation, with the purpose that each pupil may know the essence of what is Argentine, the spiritual, economic, social and political reality of his country, the evolution and historical mission of the

Argentine Republic; and so that he may acquire a consciousness of the responsibility that he should assume in the undertaking of achieving and consolidating the aims recognized and established in this Constitution.

In the light of Perón's attempts to equate Peronism and Argentine patriotism, and Sra. Perón's demands that all those opposed to the President be treated as traitors, it is not hard to imagine what direction the "political formation" envisaged in this paragraph will take.

Peronista philosophy is reflected in changes which were made in the definition of the right to private property. The Constitution of 1853 was frankly liberal in its economic outlook. It proclaimed that "Property is inviolable, and no inhabitant of the Nation can be deprived thereof except by virtue of a sentence founded on law." The Peronista Constitution, in contrast, discusses the right to hold private property in the following vein:

Private property has a social function and, in consequence, it shall be subject to the obligations that the law may establish for the purpose of the common good. It is incumbent on the State to control the distribution and utilization of the land and to intervene with the object of developing and increasing its yield, in the interests of the community, and to ensure for each rural worker or working family the possibility of becoming the owner of the land which he works.

The Peronista Constitution provides for much more active participation by the state in economic activities. It states that foreign trade "shall be in the hands of the State in accordance with the limitations and rulings that may be established by law," and labels as "the imprescriptible and inalienable property of the Nation" all such resources as "minerals, waterfalls, petroleum fields, coal-fields, gas deposits and other natural sources of energy, with the exception of vegetable resources." It specifies that "public services" are to be state-owned, and that "those which are in private possession shall be transferred to the State, by means of purchase or expropriation with prior indemnity, when such is determined by a national law." With these exceptions, "all economic activity shall be organized in accordance with free private enterprise."

The nationalism of the Peronistas is reflected in the new constitution. The old document had declared all inland rivers of Argentina open to commerce by ships of all nations, but the Peronistas modified this to read "so far as is not contrary to the requirements of defense, public security or the general interest of the State, and subject to the regulations which the National authority may apply."

The 1853 Constitution was extremely liberal in its treatment of aliens. It granted them all the civil rights belonging to a citizen, and provided that they need not become citizens if they did not care to. If they so desired, however, foreigners could become naturalized Argentines after two years of permanent residence in the republic, or earlier if they so requested and could show "service to the nation." For ten years after attaining citizenship, a naturalized Argentine was free from military service.

The Peronista Constitution modified these provisions. It stated that "foreigners who enter the country without violating the laws" shall enjoy full civil rights, and that after five years they will automatically become Argentine citizens unless they expressly state that they do not wish to do so. An alien *may* be naturalized after two years' residence, if he so desires. A new paragraph was added, providing that: "The law shall establish the causes, formalities and conditions governing the granting of Argentine nationality and the withdrawal thereof, as also the expulsion of foreigners from the country." The previous exemption of naturalized citizens from military service was removed.

The increased nationalism of the Peronista Constitution was

reflected, too, in the provisions concerning the qualifications for holding public office. Whereas the former document provided that to become a deputy one must have "four years of active citizenship," this was modified to read "to have four years' exercise of citizenship for native Argentines and ten years for naturalized Argentines." In the case of senators, the requirement formerly was that one have six years' active Argentine citizenship, whereas the Peronista Constitution provided that one must be a native-born citizen of the Republic. The same kind of changes were made in the qualifications for membership on the Supreme Court and in the Cabinet.

In the new constitution, Perón has left a monument to himself. It incorporates the social legislation which he has made his banner, although it should be noted that for the most part the "social" provisions are very broadly worded precepts rather than definite guarantees to the citizen or orders to the legislator.

The nationalism characteristic of the Peronista movement is also incorporated in the document, along with a determination to permit the state a much wider range of economic activities.

Although the new constitution ostensibly leaves Argentina with a "Federal, democratic, representative" form of government, there are definite evidences of Peronismo's dictatorial bent in the strengthening of the executive at the expense of the legislative branch and of the military at the expense of the civilian. And in spite of the generally democratic wording, the test of Peronismo will not be found in the Constitution of 1949 but rather in the actions of Juan Domingo Perón and his associates. Though the constitution may make Perón appear like a socially minded modern democrat, his actions tell a different tale.

LABOR UNDER PERON

‰

THE PERÓN ADMINISTRATION has rested on three pillars: the Army, the Church, and Organized Labor. It is the last of these which has given Perón his wide popular support. Perón himself was well aware after October 17 that maintaining the support of the workers was the keystone to the continued life of his government.

The Perón regime has continued to picture itself as a "labor government." And it has undoubtedly been true that in terms of social legislation and interest of the government in labor problems, the regimes in which Perón has been the dominant influence have done much for the workers. The President in his speech on October 17, 1949, summed up what he conceived to be the accomplishments of his "labor administration":

As a government of the people, we have brought the people themselves into the government.

Men of modest means today occupy posts which in other times were reserved for the privileged, the favored or the manipulators of electoral fraud.

As a workers' government we have not only given the worker access to public office and posts of responsibility, but have assured the freedom of trade union organization and the authority of the union in the affairs of the nation.

We have made accessible to the people the road to culture and training. Thousands of working class sons are now free to decide their careers with the help of the instruction and training offered freely by the Republic to her sons.

We have made the trade union movement effective, and have aided the consolidation of the trade union movement. Proof of this is the existence of the General Confederation of Labor, a completely independent group, and the freely functioning unions —more than a thousand in number, both autonomous and federated—which carry on their activities with complete liberty.

We have raised the standard of living of the men of the people. We have offered dignified and well remunerated work to all who want it.

We have assured the health and leisure of the worker.

We have established a regime of social security which assures the future of the Argentine worker.

We have created humane conditions of life and work, thus assuring the real freedom of the human being which is based on his economic independence and not on juridical phraseology.

These boasts of Perón are at best only half the truth. Although the Peronista regime brought increased pay, social benefits, and trade unionism, it also brought an attempt to convert the labor movement into a docile tool of the government. This tightening of government control over the unions was intensified after the inauguration of "El Líder" as President of the Republic. Some independent union groups dissolved or were destroyed, a few were captured by the Peronistas, and virtually all anti-Perón unions were driven underground. The C.G.T. continuously strengthened its control over its affiliated organizations and reached out to grasp others hitherto outside its ranks.

The first important event in the labor movement after the inauguration of Perón was the dissolution of the Communist-controlled unions, in accordance with the new line of the Communist Party adopted after the defeat of February, 1946. The Communists' unions still included one organization of considerable force—the Construction Workers Union—and other smaller groups which were combative, but had no great mass support. The most important of these were the metal workers' union and the Communists' packinghouse workers' union.

When these unions went out of existence their members joined the Peronista organizations. For the most part Communist union leaders were not admitted, but the rank and file were readily accepted. The Communists defended this move on the grounds that they did not believe in dual unionism, and that they had to go where the workers were in order to influence them. The Peronistas, for their part, apparently felt that they were strong enough to "quarantine" the Communists and render them harmless in the great mass of pro-Perón workers.

The pressure on anti-Peronista unions by the government was unabated. Two instances of how deviously the government operated will suffice. The Taxicab Drivers Union of Buenos Aires was controlled by the anarchists and affiliated with the old anarchist trade union center, the Argentine Regional Labor Federation (F.O.R.A.). Since these workers strongly resented any attempt to regiment them, the municipal government of Buenos Aires cunningly promulgated an order that all taxi drivers must paint their cars the same color, wear uniforms, and in other ways submit to stricter government control. The expected resistance occurred. The anarchist union declared a general strike in October, 1946, announcing its intention to continue this strike until the city ordinance was repealed. Of course, the municipality did not retract its order, and the taxi drivers finally went back to work—provisionally, they said—early in December.

Meanwhile, a rival Peronista-controlled union of taxi drivers was established and immediately received the legal recognition of the government. This union declared that no strike existed, organized demonstrations of loyalty to Perón, agreed to abide by the rules laid down by the Buenos Aires municipality. As a result of this carefully planned situation the anarchist union was virtually destroyed and most drivers were forced to join the Peronista group.

The Federation of Shipbuilding Workers was also an anarchist-inclined group, although it was not a member of the F.O.R.A. It had contracts with most of the important ship-repairing companies of the city of Buenos Aires. Late in 1946 when these contracts ran out, the government announced that it would not allow the signing of any new contract unless it had been negotiated through the Secretariat of Labor. The Federation, which had consistently refused to have anything to do with the government labor services, fulfilled the government's expectations and refused to negotiate under these circumstances. It called a strike which lasted several months in 1946 and 1947. As a result, the Federation was very much reduced in numbers and importance.

In spite of government pressure on the maritime unions, all but one of these united in 1949 to form an independent Confederation of Maritime Unions, which immediately joined the International Transport Workers Federation. When the Confederation called a strike in May, 1950, its action was declared illegal by the government and many of its leaders were jailed. The C.G.T. hastily organized an Agrupación de Maritimos Argentinos, as a rival to the Confederation. Needless to say, the Agrupación immediately won government recognition. The government's treatment of the Confederation's strike brought protests by the International Transport Workers Federation and the International Confederation of Free Trade Unions, but these were to no avail. The strike was finally called off six weeks after it began, since the leaders became convinced they could not win out against the Peronista government.

Instances of government persecution of anti-Peronista

unions since 1946 run into the hundreds, perhaps the thousands. The following incidents are characteristic:

In La Falda in the Province of Córdoba the local affiliate of the independent Hotel and Restaurant Workers Federation (F.O.G.R.A.) considered entering the C.G.T., but decided against it. The police then occupied the union's headquarters and turned it over to the local representatives of the C.G.T.

In Santa Fe the government prohibited a Congress of an independent rural workers' union in September, 1948.

In Mar del Plata, the resort town of Buenos Aires Province, the headquarters of the local center of independent union activity, the Unión Obrera Local, was closed by the police in December, 1947. The U.O.L. was also fined 100,000 pesos by the government.

The national congress of the F.O.G.R.A. was forbidden by the government in August, 1948.

The congress of the Shipbuilders Federation was banned by the government in March, 1949.

In Rosario in April, 1950, the local authorities ruled that in order to get a hack license all taxi chauffeurs must have the approval of the C.G.T., in spite of the fact that most local hackmen belonged at the time to the independent Unión Choferes.

Some of the independent unions were captured by the Peronistas. This was the case with the Asociación Empleados de Comercio de Rosario, which had led the fight for an independent trade union program in Minister of Interior Angel Borlenghi's own Confederation of White Collar Workers of Argentina. The Rosario union was captured by the Peronistas in elections in December, 1948.

The Federación Gráfica Bonaerense and the Federación Argentina de Trabajadores de la Imprenta (F.A.T.I.), the printing trades workers' organizations in the capital and the nation respectively, had dropped out of the C.G.T. when that organization became Peronista. The Federación Gráfica, the oldest labor organization in the country, had always been more or less under Socialist influence, while the F.A.T.I., of which the Federación Gráfica Bonaerense was a part, was headed by an old syndicalist, Sebastian Marotta. In elections early in 1947 the Peronistas gained control of the Federación Bonaerense by a very narrow margin. The Buenos Aires group then took the lead in organizing a 100 percent Peronista Federación Argentina de la Imprenta to take the place of the more "doubtful" F.A.T.I. as the central organization of the country's printing trades workers.

In some cases the Peronistas organized rival unions to compete with such workers' organizations as remained anti-Peronista. They employed this tactic in the case of the Federación de Asociaciones Catolicas de Empleadas, a group of women white collar workers in Buenos Aires, organized by Monseñor Miguel de Andrea. Since its organization in the 1920's the Federación had carried on combined trade union and mutual benefit activities, and among its many services were cheap, wholesome meals, extensive medical service, vacation resorts, and adult education. In 1946 it had some twenty-five thousand members.

Since it was deemed politically unwise to treat Monseñor de Andrea's group as violently as the Socialist, Communist, and Anarchist unions were treated, the Peronistas employed the weapon of competition. A rival Federation of White Collar Workers was organized and in May, 1950, Sra. Perón herself dedicated a large new Casa de la Empleada where the new union could provide the same kind of services as those rendered by Monseñor de Andrea's group.

Despite the use of all these methods, the opposition union groups were not completely destroyed. The Socialists tenaciously maintained control over the old but decimated textile and shoemakers' unions, a small union of white collar workers, and a few others. These organizations are grouped together in the so-called Comité Obrero Argentino de Sindicatos Independientes (C.O.A.S.I.). The anarchists continued to function through the F.O.R.A. and other organizations, such as the Shipbuilders' Federation.

Although these small rival unions were no challenge to the Peronista groups, they were bothersome gadflies. They did their best to focus international attention on the condition of the Argentine trade unions, and were active in sending delegates to international labor conventions. At the organizing meetings of the International Confederation of Free Trade Unions in Geneva and London in 1949 a representative of the C.O.A.S.I. was seated in preference to the delegates from the C.G.T., whose credentials were not accepted.

Perhaps it was the C.G.T.'s rebuff at the London I.C.F.T.U. meeting which caused the Perón government to launch its final attack on the anti-Peronista unions early in April, 1950. The headquarters of both the C.O.A.S.I. and the F.O.R.A. and of all of their constituent unions were visited by the notorious Visca Congressional Committee (which had won dubious fame by closing down most opposition newspapers). The Committee seized all the records of the F.O.R.A. and the C.O.A.S.I., placed policemen in the headquarters of the two groups, and arrested anyone who tried to enter. Thus, the anti-Peronista trade unions were forced completely underground, and Perón's labor control was virtually unchallenged.

Meanwhile, the government ordered the arrest of the C.O.A.S.I.'s delegate to the London conference of the International Confederation of Free Trade Unions, Candido Gregorio, head of the old textile workers' union. Fortunately, Gregorio was notified of this on his way back to Buenos Aires from London, and so he went no further than Montevideo,

where he set up a temporary headquarters-in-exile for the
C.O.A.S.I.

As the liquidation of the anti-Peronista unions was under
way, the government severely tightened its hold on the Peronista unions themselves. First, control of the C.G.T. was made
virtually unbreakable and then, the C.G.T.'s control of its
constituent unions was made increasingly rigid.

The way in which the subjugation of the C.G.T. was assured is told elsewhere in this volume. (See the next chapter.)
The C.G.T. itself increased its power over its affiliated unions
through the use of "intervention." The idea of the Federal government "intervening" in a provincial government or even in
a private institution is familiar and accepted in Argentina.
This policy has been carried over into labor relations by the
Peronistas, and the C.G.T. has taken upon itself the power to
unseat the elected officials of a constituent union and replace
them with leaders of its own choosing.

There is no provision for such arbitrary action in either
the C.G.T.'s own constitution or in the constitutions of the
affiliated unions. However, the C.G.T. did not let the lack
of legality stand in its way and as early as the middle of 1946
it intervened in the Union of Metal Workers on the grounds
that there was excessive Communist influence in the group—
the Communists having just liquidated their own metal workers' union to join the C.G.T. affiliate. The leaders of the Union
of Metal Workers did not protest and the precedent was established.

In January, 1947, when Luis Gay was removed as head of
the C.G.T., his union, the Federation of Telephone Workers,
which he had organized and which was peculiarly loyal to
him, was "intervened" and Gay was ousted as its chief and
replaced by an appointee of the C.G.T. Autonomy had not
been restored to this union three and a half years later.

From that time on, whenever there was a serious strike by

a C.G.T. affiliate, the C.G.T. intervened in the union involved and replaced its leadership. Such interference occurred, for instance, in the case of the Bank Workers Federation, the Graphic Workers Federation of Buenos Aires, the Sugar Workers Federation of Tucumán, and the Provincial Federation of Workers of Tucumán. Generally, the intervention lasted for a matter of years, and it was not until there was absolutely no possibility that an administration critical of the C.G.T. leadership could come into power that self-government was restored to the "intervened" union.

There is no doubt that the C.G.T. is little more than the creature of the Perón government. The ease with which the General Council of the Confederation ousted two of its executive secretaries on the mere demand of the President of the Republic is clear-cut proof. There is even more direct evidence. As early as November, 1946, this writer made an analysis of the membership of the General Council of the C.G.T. He found that of ninety-nine members at least one third either held a government job of some sort, held a position in Congress (where continuance in office depended on the President's favor) or came from unions which were either subsidized or directly intervened by the government.

The official organ of the Confederation, *C.G.T.*, clearly reflects the group's subservience to the Perón government. Taking at random a copy of that periodical—the number of March 17, 1950—we find that of the 55 articles (and continuations of articles), 31 concerned Perón, Sra. Perón, Colonel Mercante, some other government official, or a discussion of some feature of the program of the Perón government. Only 21 of the items consisted of news of individual unions or of the C.G.T.; and most of these were very short pieces, notices rather than articles. There was one article apiece concerning the International Labor Organization, the Ministry of Labor, and foreign labor movements.

In terms of column space, 76 out of the 100 columns in this issue deal with Perón, Sra. Perón, Mercante, some other government official, or a discussion of some part of the Perón government program; only 18 columns deal with news about the trade union activities of the C.G.T. and its affiliates, while three and a half columns are devoted to the I.L.O., two to foreign labor news, and half a column to official news from the Ministry of Labor. Of the 23 photographs in this issue, eleven show Perón, his wife, the Minister of Labor, or a Peronista demonstration of some kind. Two are pictures of union conventions, two deal with a visit by Chilean unionists to Argentina, while four are of C.G.T. officials. This issue of the paper, as do most issues, gives evidence that at least two pages are taken up with handouts from government ministries.

It is noteworthy that there are virtually never any notices of strikes in the *C.G.T.* The reason for this is simple: most strikes do not have the blessing of the government labor organization. In the years after the inauguration of President Perón there were several walkouts by affiliates of the C.G.T., but virtually none of these had the support of the central labor body.

The C.G.T. was unable to lure several of the important Argentine unions into its ranks. The most powerful of the abstainers was the Packinghouse Workers Federation. Despite the fact that this group was born during the *de facto* regime and had Perón for its godfather, it nevertheless clung to a certain degree of autonomy. It consistently refused to belong to the C.G.T., its leaders claiming that the Confederation was too subservient to the government. It asserted its independence by maintaining friendly relations with both the A.F.L. and C.I.O. in the United States. The C.G.T. had nothing but violent epithets for these two organizations.

Several times during the Perón administration the Packinghouse Workers engaged in bitter strikes which had something less than complete and enthusiastic support from the government. The first of these walkouts began in September, 1946. Some interpreted it at the time as a political move on the part of the government to break the backbone of elements which might be friendly to the independent aspirations of Cipriano Reyes. The strike was called to force the reinstatement of certain discharged workers, and the forcing of the packinghouses to abide by the famous decree of December 1945 obliging them to pay to each employee a bonus equal to 25 percent of his wages.

The opposition tried to use this meat workers' strike as a tool against the Government, and Radical Deputy Frondizzi acted more or less as the workers' spokesman in the Chamber. He demanded a full investigation of the whole matter, and urged the government to back up the strikers.

In June, 1950, the government began a drive to crush the Packinghouse Workers Federation. It induced several members of the Executive Committee of that organization to resign and to announce that the leaders of the Federation no longer represented the rank and file of the workers. The Minister of Labor immediately announced that he was withdrawing legal recognition from the Federation, since it no longer had the backing of the workers in the industry. The C.G.T. simultaneously set up a "Junta Intersindical de la Carne" (Inter-Union Packinghouse Committee) to organize a rival union. When no one would join the "Junta," the C.G.T. intervened in the Federación, in spite of the fact that it was not affiliated to the C.G.T. This treatment of the packinghouse workers meant an outright break between President Perón and the oldest and at one time the staunchest of his labor union supporters.

Other unions engaged in important unauthorized walkouts which incurred the displeasure of the "labor government."

In March, 1948, the bank workers walked out for several days. The reason: a delegation sent to see and present grievances to the Secretary of Labor and Perón was routed by the police and several of its members were seriously hurt. The walkout was declared illegal by the Secretary of Labor and by the leaders of the Asociación Bancaria, the legally recognized union. The members of the Inter-Bank Committee, which was running the strike, were arrested and brought before Sra. Perón, who soundly scolded them for acting so "badly" toward such a "good government." In reply they reminded her of various promises which had been made to the bank workers and which had not been kept. They finally agreed to order a return to work, pending action by Sra. Perón to honestly investigate the bank workers' grievances. However, several hundred of those most active in the strike were not allowed to return to work.

The Federación Gráfica Bonaerense was another important Peronista-controlled group to go out on strike against the wishes of the government. This union, the oldest in Argentina, closed the newspapers of the capital throughout the month of February, 1949. At a meeting on January 30, 1949, the members repudiated an agreement negotiated by the union's Peronista leadership and the Ministry of Labor, and resolved on a strike. The resignation of the union officials who had negotiated the repudiated agreement was demanded and received by the membership. The government in retaliation declared the walkout illegal, ordered the headquarters of the union seized by the police, forbade any further meetings of the strikers, and had the C.G.T. name Cecilio Conditti as "interventor" in the union.

The strike lasted for a month. The opposition papers *La Prensa* and *La Nación* signed quickly on the strikers' terms but the Peronista press held out and the walkout finally collapsed. That the government distrusted these workers and feared subsequent uprisings is demonstrated by the fact that a year and a half later the union was still "intervened."

Among the strongly pro-Perón unions which defied the leaders of both the government and the C.G.T. probably the most surprising was the Federation of Sugar Workers of Tucumán. These workers, organized largely through the efforts of Perón, owed their greatly improved wages and working conditions to their union activity. Their organization seemed particularly "safe" from the Peronista point of view since it received a subsidy from the government for "social welfare activities."

However, in spite of all this, the Federation of Sugar Workers of Tucumán (F.O.T.I.A.) declared a strike late in 1949. The walkout seriously interfered with the harvest and received a great deal of support by unions both in Tucumán and in other parts of Argentina, and finally the Federation of Workers of Tucumán declared a general strike of one day in support of the walkout. This general strike was averted by the police who arrested most of the labor leaders involved, including the head of the bakers, Carlos Antonio Aguirre. When Aguirre, a distinguished figure in the local trade union movement, did not return home when the rest of the arrested trade union leaders were released, widespread suspicion was aroused. The unions demanded to know what had become of him, but no clarification of the mystery was forthcoming from the police.

Finally, his body was discovered in a ditch in another province, a hundred miles away. Investigation revealed that he had been beaten to death by the police, and even the C.G.T. was moved to come out and condemn his murder. Several police officials were finally arrested on suspicion of killing Aguirre. They were released in July, 1950.

Although the Sugar Workers Federation did not openly attack the government, it explained the strike on the grounds that the workers of Tucumán were "dying of hunger." The Federation was bitter in denouncing some Peronista politicians, and accused Peronista Provincial Deputy Barrionuevo of Tucumán of assaulting two strikers.

The Tucumán strike is particularly interesting because of the government's attempt to lay the blame on alleged "betrayals" by local leaders. After the two unions involved in the walkout were "intervened," the C.G.T. published an "exposé," claiming that many of the leaders active in the strike had been members of the opposition, particularly of the Radical and Communist parties. Whether or not this was actually so remains in some doubt. The significant fact is that for virtually the first time the Peronistas openly admitted that a large organization in their labor group has been infiltrated by unfriendly elements.

In an effort to placate the sugar workers, when the strikers finally went back to work the President announced that he was personally seeing to it that they receive a 60 percent wage increase. Other steps were taken to regain their favor.

The most serious strike by a Peronista union was that of the members of Unión Ferroviaria in January, 1951. It was an unauthorized wildcat strike, and was preceded by two others by the same workers in November and December, 1950. The first of these was caused by demands of the workers for wage increases and was ended when the desired boosts were granted by the Minister of Transport, Colonel Castro.

Three weeks later, in December, the workers on the roads going in and out of Buenos Aires walked out again, claiming that the November agreement had not been honored by the government. This time, the strikers demanded the resignation of Unión Ferroviaria officials, claiming that they had done nothing to get the workers their desired wage hikes and had acted more like representatives of the railroad management than leaders of the union. Unión Ferroviaria President Pablo López and his assistants resigned, and soon afterwards the C.G.T appointed an interventor to conduct new elections.

By the third week in January the agreements of November and December still had not been applied, so the Emergency Consultative Committee which had led the earlier walkouts submitted an ultimatum to the government. When this was not answered, the Committee called a third walkout, demanding the promised wage boosts and that the conduct of the elections in Unión Ferroviaria be turned over to the Committee, so that López or someone like him would not again be imposed on the union. Railroad workers from all over Argentina answered the strike call.

This time the government moved quickly to break the walkout. It was declared illegal by the Ministry of Labor. Perón had already fired Colonel Castro, charging him with "betrayal" for having dealt with the rank and file strike committee in the November and December walkouts. The President summoned the C.G.T. Central Committee into session in the Executive Mansion. He demanded the approval of the C.G.T. for a decree putting into application the 1948 law which permitted the President "in case of national emergency" to draft workers "for national service" under military discipline. The C.G.T. obediently gave its rubber stamp to the decree.

On January 25 this decree was issued, and hundreds of railroad workers were arrested. Most of them were held incommunicado for two weeks and then were remanded for trial on charges of "sedition," many of them on no other grounds than membership in one of the opposition political parties. Meanwhile, two thousand railroad workers were fired. Most of the rest returned to their jobs on January 26, and service returned to normal.

Both the President and his wife were bitter in their denunciations of the railroad workers during this strike. Sra.

Perón went from station to station making screaming appeals to the workers not to "betray" her. The President accused the railroaders of gross ingratitude, saying that he had given them everything they had asked for, that the only thing he had not given them was the moon, and the only reason he hadn't given them that was that they had not asked for it.

The Unión Ferroviaria strike was certainly the most serious break which Perón had had hitherto with the ranks of Peronista organized labor. So serious was it that Perón apparently felt he would have to create a diversion to take the workers' minds off his strikebreaking. The only thing sensational enough for this purpose was to close down one of the great anti-Peronista dailies—and the railroad strike is undoubtedly the explanation for Perón's move against *La Prensa,* a move which he had hesitated to take heretofore and which was bound to arouse world public opinion against his regime.

The growing strike wave highlighted Perón's unexpected difficulty in converting the trade unions of Argentina into a monolithic "labor front." Although the top leadership of the C.G.T. was pretty completely a puppet of the government, individual unions both inside and outside the Confederation still had certain ideas of independence and autonomy.

By 1951 there was no secret of the government's growing aversion to strikes and other independent action by the workers. Increasingly the need for greater production was emphasized. In September, 1949, the administration launched a campaign against workers' absenteeism and at the same time the provincial government of Salta approved the establishment of special factory police—a move the opposition claimed was planned to stifle trade union activity by the workers.

The fate of the Argentine trade union movement has become a key to the continuance of the Perón regime, as evidences of defection in the other groups which have supported the regime—the Army and the Church—have become apparent. Important in this connection is the question of how much independence of mind the Peronista trade unionists have been able to maintain. A careful reading of some of the principal periodicals of these unions indicates that in spite of all the government and C.G.T. pressure, at least some are still chiefly concerned with the welfare and interests of their own members. They devote most of their space to discussions of the activities of their union members and mention Perón and Peronismo only in passing. Of course, these latter subjects are given space sufficient to indicate that publicly, at least, the organs are still Peronista; but they are mentioned sparingly enough to indicate that their main interest is trade union activity, not Peronista politics.

Where will the workers who become disillusioned in Perón go, politically? Many of them will probably go Communist. The Communists have, without doubt, done a better job of infiltrating into the ranks of the Peronista unions than have the other political parties. They are reportedly of considerable influence in such unions as the sugar workers of Tucumán, the printing trades' workers of Buenos Aires, and others. Perhaps the nomination by the Communists of the old Communist packinghouse workers' leader, José Peter, as candidate for governor of the province of Buenos Aires in the 1950 elections was not entirely accidental. It is known that important employers, among them many Peronistas, were by the middle of 1950 becoming increasingly worried by the apparent growth of Communist influence among the workers.

The kind of slogans and appeals used by Perón have made the transition from Peronista to Communist a comparatively simple one for disillusioned followers of "El Líder." Perón and his wife have been particularly zealous in their attempt to arouse class feeling, and, although Perón has talked of a "third front" opposed to both Communism and capitalism, he has devoted a good deal more bitterness and invective to his discussions of the evils of the latter than to his comments on the former.

Moreover, the Peronistas and their chief, in particular, have made frequent violent attacks upon the United States as a stronghold of the malefactors of great wealth and as a plutocratic, imperialistic nation. That this harangue involves a subtle degree of blackmail of Uncle Sam is not understood by the generally unsophisticated Peronista workers. To them the issue is merely that the Communists and Perón agree completely on the nefariousness of the United States. The Communists do not hesitate to point out that the only trouble with Perón is that he has not carried out his own program—and that they, in fact, are better Peronistas than Perón.

A factor which may be decisive in determining the political path ex-Peronistas will take is the growingly repressive attitude of the government. If the administration were to allow those trade union leaders who turn against the regime to organize their own political groups, remain apolitical, or return to one of the traditional parties, it is unlikely that the Communists would gain a great deal. Many of the old-line Peronistas in the unions—both members and leaders—were Socialists or Radicals before they became Peronistas. It is not unlikely that some will be inclined to return to their first political loves. Others may follow the road of Cipriano Reyes and try to strike out on an independent path.

Among the leadership of the Argentine trade union movement are many who will be likely to refuse the blandishments of the Communists. Particularly in the older unions, the leaders have fought with the Communists for decades, know how they act and what they really stand for. However, if all opposition is made illegal, in the trade union movement as well as in the country at large, the chances of the Communists will be enhanced tremendously. They are better organized and better equipped dogmatically for underground work than are followers of more democratic points of view, as was amply demonstrated in Nazi-dominated Europe. Totalitarian Communism will be better able to fight Totalitarian Peronismo than will more democratic political groups.

However, it must be remembered that politics in Latin America is extremely volatile, though less so in Argentina than in most other countries of the region. One would be foolhardy to predict what will actually happen if Perón begins to slip seriously in the estimation of the Argentine workers. The events will have to be left to speak for themselves.

EVITA

❦

FORTUNES have risen and fallen during the Perón administration. But none rose so swiftly or has stayed so high as that of the President's wife, Sra. María Eva Duarte de Perón. Although women have not been without influence in Argentine politics in previous times, no other member of the "weaker" sex has played such an outstanding role in the country's affairs of state.

"Evita" Perón, as she is familiarly called in Argentina, is about five feet five, but appears taller because she wears her hair artfully arranged in an "upsweep." She has dark brown eyes, blonde hair with reddish tints, and a startlingly white skin (partly natural and partly the result of the skillful use of make-up). Milton Bracker has commented that she "can be equally impressive in a strapless evening gown, a two-piece light print or floppy slacks." Friends and enemies are in agreement that Eva Perón is a woman of great personal fascination.

The First Lady of Argentina was born in 1919, the daughter of a small Buenos Aires provincial landowner who died early in his daughter's life. Left with but little means of support, the family moved to the city of Junín where Sra. Duarte became the proprietor of a small boardinghouse. The eldest of three daughters, Elisa, soon went to work, while Evita continued the life of a schoolgirl.

After two years of high school, Evita decided that Junín was too provincial, and, with her heart set upon being an actress, she departed with high hopes for the nation's capital and artistic center, Buenos Aires. She had little preparation for her chosen vocation, and it was some time before she finally succeeded in landing an inconsequential position as a sustaining artist on Radio Belgrano, one of the city's principal radio stations. This is the job she had when the June 4 Revolution occurred. She was at the time earning about 150 pesos a month.

In the wake of the revolution, Evita's advancement was rapid. She was on very friendly terms with a number of the leading figures in that upheaval, including the Acting President, General Ramírez. By the end of 1943 her monthly salary at Radio Belgrano had increased to 5,000 pesos and two years later she was earning 35,000 pesos a month at the *same* job.

A strikingly beautiful young lady, Eva Duarte came to know most of the military leaders then at the head of the Argentine government. It is said that she first met her future husband during a reception at Radio Belgrano in November, 1943, which was attended by leading figures in the government as well as by some of the country's principal artistic and theatrical people.

At this time, Colonel Perón had just assumed the post of Secretary of Labor and Social Welfare and was busy encouraging the organization of trade unions. He found in the pert young actress a willing associate, and Eva Duarte took a leading part in the organization of a national union of radio employees. In this role she no doubt gained experience which was to prove useful later when she became, for practical purposes, Minister of Labor.

Meanwhile her relationship with Colonel Perón became increasingly close, and her fate became bound to his. So much was this true that during the period of Perón's ousting in October, 1945, Eva Duarte was fired from her lucrative job with Radio Belgrano. She thereupon helped organize the workers' movement responsible for the events of October 17. A few days after his reinstatement Colonel Perón married the 26-year-old radio actress.

With the inauguration of her husband as President of the Republic, Evita began to play an increasingly important part in the nation's public affairs. Putting her talents as a radio performer to work, she aided her husband in the so-called "Battle of Sixty Days" against inflation. She went on the air to announce ceiling prices for clothing and to give hints to housewives on ways to economize. In the first of these appearances, she was introduced by the Secretary of Industry and Commerce who compared her with Mrs. Roosevelt.

At this time she had her office on the fourth floor of the Central Post Office, where she was assisted by a battery of technical experts and secretaries. Her audiences on Monday, Wednesday, and Friday were besieged by people of all ranks and occupations who came to tell their tales of woe or to ask favors. She thus began to build up her own popular following. The writer recalls speaking with a group of leaders of the Trolley-Car Workers Union in Rosario in November, 1946, who were aglow with enthusiasm for Sra. Perón. On a visit to their headquarters, she had shown a great deal of interest not only in their trade union problems but in their families and their living conditions.

Increasingly she toured the interior, going to out-of-the-way places which her husband was too busy to visit, speaking before trade unions, and propagandizing her husband's fight for the "descamisados" ("the shirtless," a term for Perón's followers which she was credited with having coined during the 1946 election campaign). Her beauty, her youth, and her obvious proletarian origin all helped to win her supporters in her own right.

Her "nouveau riche" penchant for wearing quantities of jewelry and expensive clothes did not weaken her popular support, as it might have been expected to do. In fact, she adroitly used her stylishness as a political weapon during the 1946 presidential campaign. In a speech she pointed to her own beautifully dressed self as a symbol of Argentine opportunities, saying: "You will all have clothes like these some day. . . . Some day you will be able to sit next to any rich woman on a basis of complete equality. What we are fighting for is to destroy the inequality between you and the wives of your bosses." Her clothes were Argentine-made before she became the First Lady of the Land, but subsequently she had them made by Christian Dior of Paris.

During the early months of the Perón administration Evita carried on an active campaign for women's suffrage, which had been promised in the Peronista platform. In February, 1947, she bought control of the Peronista newspaper *Democracia* and thereafter wrote a daily column, "The Argentine Woman Wants to Vote." Subsequently she bought control of two other Buenos Aires dailies, *Noticias Gráficas* and *Laborista*. By this time she was also said to "indirectly control" all the newsreel companies, no doubt the reason that she never failed to appear two or three times in each newsreel sequence. She also had a regular broadcasting spot each Wednesday night, on which her main theme was also women's suffrage.

A few months after these first political excursions, Sra. Perón tried her hand—quite successfully—at foreign affairs. In those days Perón was maintaining particularly close relations with Generalissimo Franco, while at the same time posing as the great humanitarian making sizable loans to various of Argentina's customers. It was in conjunction with these two presidential policies that Evita Perón went abroad in the middle of 1947.

Her first stop was in Spain, where she spent seventeen days on a barnstorming tour up and down the country. During her stay, Evita is said to have distributed some $50,000 in cash among the eager crowds that constantly swarmed around her wherever she went. Her crowning moment was when Franco bestowed upon her the Order of Isabél La Catolica.

Proceeding to Italy, Sra. Perón was granted her desired interview with the Pope, but to her dismay did not receive an entirely favorable welcome from the Italian people. In one case a group outside the Argentine Embassy in Rome was crying "Perón! Perón! Perón!" when some toper struck up the more familiar cry of "Duce! Duce! Duce!" Countershouting then began in the crowd, "Down with Franco! Down with Perón! Down with Fascism!" Sra. Perón was described as being "upset" by this incident.

In France the Argentine President's wife was met at the airport by President and Mrs. Auriol. In the French capital she won the sobriquet "la belle blonde," but one unfriendly commentator, noting her presence at the signing of a commercial treaty by which Argentina loaned $150,000,000 to France, said, "Madame Perón will be made palatable to the French workers and peasants by being dressed as a piece of Argentine frozen beef."

Far more important than Evita Perón's soap-box campaign for women's rights or her triumphant tours, however, has been her activity in connection with organized labor. When soon after her husband's inauguration she moved her office to the Secretariat of Labor, she became for practical purposes Secretary of Labor. The titular holder of this office since 1946 has been José María Freire, an ex-official of the Glassmakers Union, who undoubtedly was chosen because of his innocuousness. Señor Freire has survived the many changes in the Perón cabinet—probably because he gets in no one's way.

Sra. Perón has extended her influence over the working class through two organisms—the trade unions (particularly the C.G.T.) and the María Eva Duarte de Perón Welfare

Foundation. The latter organization, originally established in June, 1947, has as its function the distribution of medicine, food, and money to needy people throughout the country. It is sort of a magnified Tammany Hall favor-dispenser. It has also played a significant role in international affairs, since the Foundation has frequently given gifts to workers of other Latin American countries—usually in strategic places at strategic moments. In fact, Sra. Perón did not hesitate to extend her bounty to the poor children of Washington, D.C. State Department officials there had red faces when, after Washington welfare leaders made a routine request to the Argentine Embassy (as to other embassies) for a donation, the María Eva Duarte de Perón Foundation contributed a sizable number of garments. The astounded welfare agencies at first refused the shipment and then, on the advice of the embarrassed State Department, accepted the charity "with thanks."

The following example will serve to demonstrate the kind of work the Foundation does and the favorable political effect of its operations. A violent strike of sugar workers in the province of Tucumán in December, 1949, was broken by the government with the help of the C.G.T., which "intervened" in the union, putting in charge people more amenable to orders from Buenos Aires. Perón then granted a belated 60 percent wage increase to the ex-strikers, but anti-government feeling still ran high.

A few months later, Sra. Perón's Foundation sent sizable amounts of clothing to the workers of the province, to be distributed by the local representative of the C.G.T. The apparent aim—to improve the standing of both the Peróns and the C.G.T.—was evidently achieved. The organ of the Confederation, *C.G.T.*, noted that:

The distribution of clothes gave rise to scenes of extraordinary enthusiasm, during which there were excited and clamorous cheers

for Sra. Perón and for the Leader of the Workers, General Juan
Perón. Just before the distribution of the clothing, the delegate
from the C.G.T. gave an enthusiastic speech in which he pointed
out the altruistic, generous and patriotic action of Comrade Evita,
whose heart is full of sympathy and love towards her fellow
humans.

The C.G.T. delegate is further quoted as saying:

In this era of Argentina's recovery, there is one star in the nation's
sky which constantly guides the destinies of the humble and the
disinherited, bringing them counsel and aid. . . . This star which
lights the homes of the humble is our comrade Evita, Eva Perón,
the woman who stands at the side of the Leader, representing the
Country itself.

Other activities of the Foundation include the organization of sports championships and other public events.

The sources of funds are various. Much of the money comes
from the trade unions. In 1949 the railroad workers "spon-
taneously" donated to the Foundation 50 percent of an increase received in a new collective contract—a contribution
which amounted to some 12,000,000 pesos. The Unión Pe-
trolera at the same time was reported as giving 450,000
pesos, the Unión Obreros Municipales, 7,000,000, and the
Trolley-Car Workers Union, 6,000,000 pesos. Lesser contribu-
tions were being made by other unions from time to time. A
somewhat different source was disclosed in 1948 when it was
announced that John Montague Edy was submitting 100,000
pesos in the name of the British ex-owners of the Argentine
railroads. The opposition claimed that the Banco Central
requested all of its employees to give one day's pay to the
Fundación: any of the bank's employees not wishing to do so
were asked to notify their employer.

An attempt by Congress to appropriate a large sum of
money for the María Eva Duarte de Perón Foundation in
1949 was vetoed by Evita's husband. The exact motives for

his action are somewhat obscure, but it was more than likely that this was a gesture to demonstrate that there was nothing "official" about the Foundation, that it was wholly a private philanthropic venture on the part of the President's wife.

There is little or no public accounting for the funds which the Foundation receives and dispenses. There is no public record of just how much Sra. Perón has had at her command through that organization, or just what she has done with it. The opposition has insisted that the handling of the funds of the organization has been scandalous, but no investigation has been made of the charges—or is likely to be made so long as the Peróns remain the country's rulers.

In the trade unions Sra. Perón soon took over the position her husband had occupied during the days of the *de facto* government. From time to time she takes part in ceremonies surrounding the signing of important collective bargaining contracts, and hers is the ear into which the grievances of the Argentine workers are poured.

Sra. Perón's growing influence in the C.G.T. has been reflected in the decline in importance of the original Peronistas —those labor leaders who were the first civilian adherents of Perón and built up support for him among the trade unions so well that he was able to take their own followers away from them.

One by one these original Peronistas have fallen by the wayside. Luis Gay, president of the Partido Laborista, and old-time leader of the Telephone Workers, was ousted as secretary general of the C.G.T. in January, 1947, after Perón called the Executive Committee of the Confederation to the presidential palace and ordered them to depose him. His successor, Aurelio Hernández, an ex-Communist and fervent Peronista, was first praised to the skies in the *C.G.T.* and other government periodicals for a little over half a year; then he suddenly was ousted and disappeared from the public prints. The cause? A dispute with Evita.

Hernández was succeeded as C.G.T. secretary general by José Espejo. Espejo had virtually no trade union experience. One version of his previous history was that he had once been superintendent of an apartment building in which Evita resided. Those who have talked with Espejo since his becoming secretary general say that he can use up an hour's conversation with discussing what a wonderful woman Sra. Perón is. In spite of all attempts to build him up in the Peronista press, he remains a very disconsolate-looking figure.

Secretaries general of the C.G.T. were not the only trade union leaders to fall victims to the enmity of Sra. Perón. The leadership of the Unión Ferroviaria, the powerful union of railway workers, was purged in 1948. Other unions experienced the same fate.

Sometimes Sra. Perón intervenes personally in touchy labor situations. In March, 1949, she called in the leaders of the packinghouse workers' local union in Berisso in the suburbs of Buenos Aires and asked them to call off their program of having the workers labor only six hours a day. The local union had begun this procedure on its own accord—on the ground long hours were dangerous to the workers' health—after failing to persuade the local management to do so.

The Evita "house-cleaning" has moved into areas of high state policy. It was an open secret for many months that the President's wife was seeking the scalp of Juan Bramuglia, then Minister of Foreign Affairs. The Peronista press, most of which is subject to orders from Evita, did not even mention Bramuglia by name during the month when as Chairman of the Security Council of the United Nations he was trying to bring an end to the Berlin blockade. He was being mentioned for the Nobel Peace Prize in the papers of Europe and the rest of America, but he was merely referred to as "The Chancellor" in the press of Buenos Aires. He finally resigned, ostensibly as the result of a dispute with the Argentine Ambassador in Washington. Sra. Perón was on the side of the ambassador.

The key to Bramuglia's downfall is to be found in his connection with the labor movement. He had for years been lawyer for Unión Ferroviaria and had been one of Perón's chief advisers in winning support among the country's labor leaders. With the old group who had first come to Perón's support, Bramuglia undoubtedly had considerable influence, and as Sra. Perón extended her power in labor circles, Bramuglia's popularity became dangerous. She set out to eliminate it.

On the solid basis of labor support, Evita's influence has spread into other areas of the government. In March, 1950, one of her friends was named as Under Secretary of Information and a few months later the head of the Fundación Social was named a minister.

The fall from grace of Minister of Education Oscar Ivanissevich is widely attributed to Evita's dislike. Early in 1950 one of Evita's political protégés, Miel Asquia, president of the Peronista bloc in the Chamber of Deputies, failed an examination in Administrative Law in the University of Buenos Aires, where he was registered as a student. A few days later Sra. Perón called Dr. Ivanissevich and asked him to "straighten out this problem." Ivanissevich said he would be glad to arrange for another examination for Miel Asquia. This did not please Evita who demanded that her protégé be passed on the spot. This, Dr. Ivanissevich said, was impossible. The conversation ended there, but a few days later the Minister of Education surprised everyone by handing in his resignation, and it is widely felt in Buenos Aires that the Miel Asquia incident was a prime cause of his disgrace.

Not content with running the Foundation and the Ministry of Labor, the President's wife also has oversight of the Ministry of Health, an organization which has accomplished a good deal since its establishment in 1947. It has made great headway in fighting tuberculosis, malaria, and leprosy. Weekly visits were instituted to all homes in the malaria area by mosquito control teams of the Ministry. As a result, whereas in 1943 there were more than 8,000 cases of malaria in Argentina, in 1948 there were only two proven cases.

Sra. Perón's Health Ministry also has general oversight of the government's hospital program, and claims to have established one hundred hospitals in 1948 alone. The ministry has developed a considerable program of preventive medicine, with much emphasis on spreading information among schoolchildren. By 1952 the ministry plans to have established an annual health check-up for each citizen.

On the other hand it appears not unlikely that many of the restrictive measures adopted by the Perón regime against its opponents have been devised and pushed by Sra. Perón. In March, 1950, she called for the branding of all opponents of the Perón regime as traitors. Her newspaper *Democracia* defended the closing of anti-Peronista papers by the government on the grounds that Argentina was thus freed from the dictates of the newsprint importers. Observers have commented that some of the devices used against the opposition have seemed the product of feminine deviousness.

Eva Perón's increasing prominence raises the question of whether or not she has designs upon her husband's position as "Leader of the Workers." She consistently portrays herself in her speeches as the collaborator of the "Leader" and as his intermediary with the workers. However, there have been several suggestions that she may seek public office for herself. Late in May, 1950, the Entre Ríos provincial convention of the Peronista Party suggested that Sra. Perón should be "a candidate for high office" in the next elections. A year and a half earlier one Peronista newspaper had boosted Evita for governor of the Province of Buenos Aires, on the supposition that the presidential ticket in the 1952 campaign would be Perón and Mercante, for president and vice president respectively, thus leaving the Buenos Aires governorship vacant. In September, 1950, Milton Bracker reported to the New York *Times* that there was widespread belief that Evita would run for vice president when her husband seeks reelection in 1952.

However, Evita Perón herself has given little evidence that she intends to seek elective office. Hard as she battled for obtaining the right to vote for women, she has not suggested that it would be appropriate for women to seek high office. It would indeed be a bold break with Argentine tradition were she to make any such attempt.

In any case, the importance of the President's wife in the Argentine political picture is surpassed only by that of her husband, and the two have become inseparable in the public mind. She undoubtedly does much to strengthen the hold of President Perón on the group which is the key to his continuing in power—the workers. Of her popularity in working-class quarters there is little doubt. She reinforces her husband's position among the laboring classes at a time when his own standing among that group has begun to decline.

THE ARMY IN POLITICS—
PERON AND THE MILITARY

ALTHOUGH it is from the ranks of organized labor that Perón has derived his greatest popular support, it was the Army that first gave him power and it is the Army which will probably have the final say as to his retaining that power. In spite of his close association with trade unionists and ordinary workers during his rapid rise to power, Perón has remained a staunch Army man. Only five days before his inauguration as President, he was restored by his predecessor to the Army's active list and promoted from Colonel to Brigadier General.

The *coup d'état* of June 4, 1943, was essentially a military uprising, in which no important segment of the civilian population played a significant role; this was in contrast to the Revolution of 1930, which had the active cooperation of the Conservative, anti-Irigoyen Radical, and Independent Socialist parties. In the 1943 Revolution, no party came to the aid of the new regime, and it was not until Perón himself organized two groups—the Peronista Radicals and the Partido Laborista—that any organized civilian political backing was achieved.

Even when the government became "constitutional" after the inauguration of Perón as president on June 4, 1946, military men continued to play a prominent role. The Perón cabinet has consistently included several military men. The

Peronista provincial governors have included Colonel Mercante in the Province of Buenos Aires, Colonel San Martín in Córdoba, General Velazco in Corrientes, Colonel García in Tucumán, General Albariño in Entre Ríos, and Colonel Brisoli in Mendoza. Brisoli was elected only after a contest with another military man within the Peronista party.

Other important civilian jobs, such as the chief of the Railroad Administration and the head of the National Energy Administration, have been held by Army officers. Throughout the Perón regime the head of the Federal Police has consistently been a military man. Positions within the Peronista Party itself are very frequently held by military figures, and Admiral Teisaire served a long term as the party's president.

There are two main reasons for this predominance. In the first place, of course, it is good politics, as the armed forces are the only group in Argentina capable of overthrowing President Perón. One way to safeguard the regime is to give military men many of the best jobs available in the state apparatus. In the second place, Perón's personal preferences are no doubt responsible to a considerable degree for this plethora of military faces in the ranks of his administration. He was a career Army man. For many years his closest friends and associates were men who came from the barracks. His outlook is that of a military man.

Perón has never apologized for the leading role which militarists have played in recent Argentine political history. Indeed, in a speech given on December 4, 1943, he developed the idea that military revolution is in the nature of a constitutional phenomenon. In flowery terms he declared the Army to be the moral reserve of the nation, and stated that at the time of the June 4, 1943, upheaval "virtue had flown to the barracks."

Years later, in a speech to the Artillery School, Perón presented other aspects of what he considers the role of the military in public life:

Government is a struggle, and struggles—be they military or economic—are governed by the same principles. A fight is always a fight. And that is the advantage which we soldiers have over other people, we know the techniques and can better carry out a fight. We are better qualified than any other group to win in such a struggle. The rest may have the intelligence, but the spirit of struggle and the decision to conquer, come what may, is more highly developed in the soldier than in members of any other profession.

These are not the statements of a man who feels that the military should not participate in active politics. In addition to the appointment of high-ranking officers to important civilian posts, the Perón regime encouraged interest in the selection of government among the lower ranks when it pushed through Congress a law giving non-commissioned officers the right to vote. (It is interesting to note, in view of Perón's campaign in favor of the "descamisados" that the law did *not* give the franchise to privates, however.)

The military orientation of the regime is further indicated in the law, passed in August, 1948, giving the government dictatorial powers in case of war or "a grave emergency." Among these powers is the right to replace provincial civil governors with military governors.

The influence of the military on civilian life has increased greatly in the economic realm as well as in politics. An important part of the industrialization program of the Perón Five Year Plan—including the establishment of an iron and steel industry—has been put under the aegis of the Ministry of Defense. Already existing military factories have greatly increased their capacity. The Military Airplane Factory, for instance, increased its staff from about 1,000 to 5,000 between 1943 and 1949.

The colonels and generals who have become cabinet ministers and provincial governors are not the only ones to materially benefit from the Perón administration. The average officer has seen his pay raised to unprecedented heights. For example, a married subaltern (2d Lieutenant) in the Army in 1945 was reported to receive about 375 pesos, plus 51 pesos for food; in 1949 an officer of the same class received 1,100 pesos total pay and rations. The New York *Herald Tribune* reported in 1948 that the Argentine officer as a rule received more pay than his opposite number in the United States Army. The comparative salary scales, as given by the *Herald Tribune,* are shown, in dollars, in Table 2:

TABLE 2

Rank	United States	Argentina
Lieutenant General	8,800	11,250
Major General	8,800	10,000
Brigadier General	6,600	8,750
Colonel	4,400	7,000
Lt. Colonel	3,850	5,500
Major	3,300	4,250
Captain	2,760	3,250
First Lieutenant	2,400	2,500
Second Lieutenant	2,160	2,125

The *Herald Tribune* noted that allowances for rations and quarters were about the same in the two armies. But if an Argentine officer was sent to the United States for official business, his salary in Argentine pesos was converted into the same number of dollars (the exchange at the time was from 4–5 pesos to $1): a temporary pay rise which the traveling military men of the United States certainly did not receive.

These pay increases are but one explanation for the very great expansion in military expenditures during the Perón regime. A large increase in the manpower of the Army un-

doubtedly occurred between 1943 and 1949, just how large
it is difficult to tell. Juan Antonio Solari, a Socialist leader
who has been particularly interested in this, said in 1946 that
the Army had grown from about forty thousand at the time
of the 1943 Revolution to over one hundred thousand. That
this estimate was probably not far from wrong is indicated
by the fact that President Perón himself reported in 1949 that
the Army had been cut from a high of 105,000 in 1945 to
70,000 four years later.

Much of the inflated military budget has been spent on
equipment and construction of military installations. In this
connection, President Perón announced, in the middle of
1949, that the Army had reached a "satisfactory state of
modernization," achieved, he said, in part through purchases
abroad, but increasingly the country had been able to supply
its military needs through use of Argentina's own productive
resources. There is some doubt about the degree to which
such an increase has really occurred, and it seems reasonable
to suppose that since 1943 a sizable part of the country's
foreign exchange has gone to purchase military equipment.

The exact extent of this "modernization" of the Argentine
armed forces is unknown, but it is common knowledge that
the Air Force boasts four-engined Lincoln bombers and at
least 100 Gloucester meteor jet fighters which were purchased from Great Britain. No other Latin American air force
possesses these advanced weapons of war.

The military budget has been immense. It was estimated
that in the 1950 budget military expenses accounted for
25 percent of the whole. In the fiscal year 1949 the three
ministries of War, Marine, and Aviation had a total original
budget of 1,021 million pesos, to which should be added 329
million pesos for autonomous organs of the three ministries.
The sum of 309 millions were appropriated for the Ministry
of National Defense and 45 millions for payment of retire-

ment and pensions to ex-soldiers, sailors, and airmen. Moreover, on July 24, 1948, extraordinary credits of 150 millions a year were passed to cover salary increases: eight millions for the National Gendarmerie, one million more for the Navy, 34 millions for the Federal Police; eight millions for the personnel of defense and security forces in the national territories. An additional 16 millions was also provided for the Dirección General de Gendarmeria, and almost three millions for the Bureau of Land Construction of the Ministry of the Navy.

Later in the fiscal year, some 500 million pesos were provided for the Bureau of Military Factories and additional credits were approved thus: 54 millions for the Ministry of War, 45 millions for the Ministry of Navy, and 25 millions for the Ministry of Aviation. The same session of Congress which passed these appropriations provided 458 millions for the construction of barracks and other military installations, plus an item of 15 percent for studies, plans, direction and control of these works.

It has been estimated that the barracks existing in 1948 would take care of three times the number of men that were under arms before the June, 1943, revolt. And it is claimed by the opposition that these military construction projects have absolute priority over civilian construction programs. The opposition paper *Reconstruir* writes that "Technical experts have indicated that the great increase in the cost of materials and consequently in the cost of homes has been due to the fact that a large part of the resources have been invested in these military construction projects."

Under Perón there has been a thorough reorganization of the military. Following in the footsteps of the world's large powers, Argentina established a fourth military ministry— the Ministry of National Defense. However, unlike most nations, Argentina did not see fit to make the three service

ministries—Army, Navy, Aviation—subservient to the Ministry of National Defense. This anomalous situation, in which
the Ministry of National Defense takes on some of the aspects
of the fourth side of a triangle, arose from interservice politics
among the military forces. As a result, General Humberto
Sosa Molina, the architect of the whole reorganization, was
isolated as Minister of National Defense, in a position where
the real power had slipped into the hands of others.

The open rivalry between the Army and Air Force in Argentina has been described as "classic," and relations between the Army and Navy are no better. In part these rival-
ries have a political origin. Although Admiral Teisaire has
played a large part in Peronista politics, and other Navy men
have held posts of importance in the administration, the Navy
has the reputation of being the service most unfriendly to
President Perón. This attitude dates from before his inauguration. On September 24, 1945, a letter signed by forty-two
Navy admirals and captains urged the return to constitutional
government, and in October, 1945, the Navy cooperated
wholeheartedly in the attempted overthrow of Perón. Today
those young men who, though anti-Peronista, want to enter
the armed forces, gravitate toward the Navy.

However, the Navy has not been entirely overlooked in the
armament program of the Peronista government. Its acquisi-
tions since 1946 have included at least three cruisers and one
aircraft carrier, and numerous landing craft and other small
vessels.

In part, the lack of harmony among the armed forces is
but the result of the natural struggle among the three services
—a situation not unknown in countries like the United States
and Britain. Such rivalry might be expected to be intensified
in a country like Argentina where the armed forces cut altogether a bigger swathe in national life. It is not unlikely,
moreover, that this rivalry is encouraged by Perón himself.

So long as the surplus energies of the three military services are used up in fighting with one another, Perón can be fairly sure that they will not join in opposition to him. Divide and rule has long been a cardinal principle of politicians, and Perón is without doubt the wiliest politician in Argentina—perhaps Latin America—today.

Such a policy is certainly not without merit, from Perón's point of view. There have been evidences that the military are becoming restless and in a country where the Army giveth, the Army can also take away. The Perón administration has already been threatened by several crises in the relations between the government and the armed forces. At one time a rumor was circulated in Buenos Aires that the G.O.U. had ordered Perón to either solve the growing economic crisis or step down.

Another crisis centered on Miguel Miranda, the "economic wizard" of the early part of the Perón administration. The Army was not particularly fond of Señor Miranda, perhaps because he was the chief civilian figure of importance in the administration and his influence with the President rivaled that of the military men themselves. In part, too, they felt he was mixing into affairs which were more the concern of the military than of the president of the Banco Central.

The Army and Miranda waged a bitter fight over the building of a tin-plate plant. The Army thought that this should be in their province, as was the National Steel Plant which they were authorized to establish under the Five Year Plan. Señor Miranda, on the other hand, wanted to have charge of that part of the country's industrialization program. After a long-drawn-out feud, the military finally won, and Miranda dropped the whole matter. For some time there was fear that this might cause the military to turn against the whole regime.

Sra. Perón herself became a bone of contention between the Army and her husband, and on one occasion almost caused an open break. The military leaders are not particularly fond of the lovely Evita and resent particularly her great activity in Argentine public affairs. It is reported that in 1948 they demanded that she retire from political activity: for several weeks after their ultimatum her public appearances were limited and on some of these occasions she made no speech. The Army's enmity became unmistakable when twice during the month of February, 1949, Sra. Perón tried to visit the Campo de Mayo army base outside of Buenos Aires and was—like any other civilian—unceremoniously turned away by the sentry. Appeals by Evita to her husband and by him to the Army authorities were to no avail. General Humberto Sosa Molina, head of the armed forces, stood firm and even refused to leave the Army headquarters at Campo de Mayo.

These unfriendly relations were finally smoothed over, and to mark the end of "hostilities" President and Sra. Perón were entertained at Campo de Mayo at a formal banquet given by the officers of the garrison. Toasts were drunk to the health of all, and Perón, Evita, and General Sosa Molina all made speeches. Afterwards General Sosa Molina distributed to his fellow officers an impressive thirty-page booklet containing the speeches which he and the President had made at the dinner given "in honor of the President and of his wife Doña María Eva Duarte de Perón."

The threat of Army dissatisfaction continually haunts the administration, but it is unlikely that Perón's fears will become reality for some time to come. There are several reasons. First of all, the Army for the only time in its history is enjoying popularity among the great masses of the people. Argentina has not fought any wars for nearly eighty years, and the Army before 1943 had become largely an overgrown police force. Its reactionary outlook caused it to be not at all beloved by civilians, and particularly disliked by organized workers.

With the coming of Perón to power, however, the Army basked in his reflected glory. He was popular, some of his oldest collaborators in the Army ranks—such as Mercante, Velasco—were also well-liked, and as a result the whole Army tended to experience public approval for the first time. There can be little doubt that the Army likes the friendly support it receives from the people, particularly from the workers. It relishes being called "our army comrades" instead of being regarded with hate.

In the second place, the Army seems to entertain a healthy respect for the power of Perón's labor legions. The workers are unarmed but fanatical, and are capable of paralyzing all activity for a longer or shorter period. Furthermore, they would not hesitate to turn out in their hundreds of thousands and take control of Buenos Aires—as they did on October 17 —if called upon to do so by their "Líder." No doubt the Army could restore "order," but only at the price of great carnage and violence. The Argentine Army would again become violently hated by the masses of the people, and the man the regime had overthrown would become a national martyr.

Finally, the Army's high command is aware of the President's considerable support among the rank and file of the armed forces. This is said to have been one of the reasons why the Army ended its feud with Perón early in 1948. Certainly the common soldiers would have no particular liking for fighting Argentine workers.

Therefore, it seems that until the support of Perón among the working classes is seriously weakened, the Army will not attempt a revolt. It will not risk a clash with hundreds of thousands of determined workers, a clash which it could undoubtedly win, but which would be detrimental to its interests for years to come, perhaps for generations.

CHURCH AND STATE IN PERON'S ARGENTINA

ARGENTINA is nominally a Catholic country. The overwhelming majority of the population are baptized in the Church and receive its other sacraments. Roman Catholicism is the state religion.

Yet, as early as 1884 those Argentines who favored a more secular society bested the supporters of the established Church in the field of education. By the famous law of that year it was decided—presumably once and for all—that education in the state-supported schools would be secular and that, although Catholic schools would not be forbidden, there would be no teaching of religion in the government-run educational institutions. Virtually everyone took the issue for granted, and in the succeeding decades clericalism and anticlericalism were hardly a serious factor in Argentine politics.

All this was changed in 1943. The trend of more than a half century was reversed with the formation of an alliance between the Peronistas and the Church hierarchy in Argentina. This alliance cannot be documented, and it is doubtful if it was ever set down on paper. Nevertheless, the evidence is sufficient to indicate that some kind of an understanding existed between the high Argentine Catholic officials and the Peronista leaders.

Objection may be taken to this analysis on the grounds that

it is the general policy of the Roman Church to support duly constituted governments, and that the Church hierarchy's backing of Perón is nothing more than the faithful execution of this policy. However, the aid which the Catholic Church officials have given to Perón has been more than just the patriotic support of their government by good Argentine Catholics. It has been political support of Perón by high officials of the Church, who presumably speak in its name within their jurisdictions.

The crux of the understanding between the Church and the leaders of the military regime seems to have been the reestablishment of compulsory Catholic religious instruction in government schools which was brought about by a decree of December, 1943. Reaction was widespread, but more or less futile. There was strong opposition among the teachers, and a number of them resigned rather than teach under such circumstances. The issues boiled and bubbled beneath the surface for three years. A nation-wide Congress for Secular Education was held in December, 1946, in which Radical and Socialist and non-party educators and political figures participated. At about the same time final approval was given to this educational measure by the Peronista-controlled Congress.

Within the administration itself, the role of the clergy became an important one. Various government institutions, even the Transport Corporation of Buenos Aires which runs the trolleys and busses in that city, were given "ecclesiastical advisers." Minister of Interior Angel Borlenghi, in explaining the proposed budget for his ministry in 1949, noted an item of 100,000 pesos for "ecclesiastical expenses." Sra. Perón established a Dirección Espiritual in her Fundación Ayuda Social María Eva Duarte de Perón and named as its head Father Hernán Benítez who during the Second World War had been an advocate of Franco's "Hispanidad" program.

The general attitude of the Perón government has been one of endorsement and active support of the activities of the Church, in sharp contrast with previous regimes which more or less let the Church go its way. For example, the Perón government allowed religious parades through the streets of Buenos Aires during Easter Week, and government officials participated in them. Such demonstrations as these were virtually unknown in Argentina—at least in Buenos Aires— before the coming to power of the Perón administration.

One opposition newspaper notes that "The advance and penetration of clericalism is very noticeable. In each ward of whatever city, churches have at their disposal all possible means of propaganda. For the clergy there are no ordinances which are binding. Modern loudspeakers disturb the neighborhood with hymns, slogans, sermons."

For its part, the Church has been open in its support of the regime. The Peronistas introduced an innovation in Argentine politics, at least in Argentine labor politics, when they began the policy of having clergymen present at party meetings and rallies to give their blessing to the proceedings. As one anti-Peronista Argentine Catholic clergyman remarked to this writer, "Although the Church has not really endorsed any politician it is not hard to see how some might think that it has, since priests appear at all of the Peronista political rallies."

During the election campaign of 1945–1946 the Argentine bishops issued a pastoral letter on the election and demanded that no Catholic vote for candidates whose programs included the legalization of divorce, a ban on Church schools, or separation of Church and State. The Peronistas immediately claimed that this letter was a condemnation of the anti-Peronista Democratic Union, since every party belonging to that group advocated one or more of these forbidden planks. Some substance seemed to be lent to this assertion by the proclamation of the Bishop of Paraná, who forbade the faithful to vote for "Communists, Socialists or any party affiliated or cooperating with them." On the other hand a group of 500 Catholic laymen defied their clerical leaders and during the election campaign signed a letter denouncing Perón as a totalitarian and urging their coreligionists to vote for his opponent.

Later the Church hierarchy continued to act in ways which favored the political fortunes of the Peronista group. In September, 1948, when the government announced the discovery of a "plot" to assassinate Perón (in which ex-Peronista Cipriano Reyes and ex-United States diplomat John Griffiths were the alleged principals), the Argentine bishops took the announcement at its face value and ordered prayers of thanksgiving that Perón and his wife had escaped assassination to be said in all Argentine churches on September 26, 1948.

Some priests have been particularly active in the Peronista movement. The most notorious of these is Father Virgilio Filippo, who has a reputation for being one of the country's most vituperative orators, and who combines fanatic support for Perón with anti-Semitism and other not necessarily relevant doctrines. Padre Filippo has been a fervent worker for Perón and has frequently appeared in Perón political demonstrations. For instance, the Peronista paper *El Laborista* published a picture on July 12, 1948, of Father Filippo giving out prizes and medals to 480 workers who had done an outstanding job. He was quoted as urging the recipients to keep up the good work for the "social justice" state of Perón.

In 1948 Father Filippo was elected a Peronista member of the Chamber of Deputies, winning by the smallest majority of any on the Partido Peronista slate from the city of Buenos Aires. Although a pulpit orator of note, he has not made a very great splash as a member of the Chamber. It is significant that no attempt has been made by the Church hierarchy to muzzle him in any of his political activities.

Another Catholic clergyman, Father Arturo Melo, is an

active Peronista in the province of Catamarca and published a daily paper *La Unión.* In 1948 he and another leading Peronista of the province, Senator Vicente Saadi, had a falling out and violently attacked one another in their two newspapers. Melo accused Senator Saadi of graft in gaining his seat in the Senate: another man had first been named by the provincial legislature, then his election had been canceled and Saadi had been named in his stead—and *La Unión* gave times and places and amounts of graft. As a result, Saadi lodged two lawsuits against Father Melo, one for libel and another for "disrespect" of his senatorial toga. The Bishop of Catamarca came to the defense of Father Melo, saying that Senator Saadi was acting wrongly in making a priest subject to a suit in a civil court.

Quite different was the attitude of the hierarchy toward Father José M. Dunphy, a priest in one of the suburbs of Buenos Aires, who gained considerable attention by his strong condemnations of the regime. Father Dunphy devoted numerous sermons to such subjects as liberty and Christian democracy and indicated that he thought the Perón government was acting in opposition to these ideals. In January, 1949, Father Dunphy was removed from his parish by Cardinal Copello, and his appeals to the Papal Nuncio for a trial went unheeded.

Other clerics have also opposed President Perón and his administration, though usually not with the frankness which marked Father Dunphy's behavior. Outstanding among the recognized opponents of the administration has been Monseñor Miguel de Andrea, Bishop of Temnos, and only Argentine bishop who did not sign the pastoral letter in favor of Perón's election in 1945. (He was not called upon to do so since his see is not in Argentina but is a more or less mythical one in the Near East.) He issued a statement during the campaign warning the workers not to sell their freedom for "a handful of benefits," and he added, "Class hatred is being set on fire dangerously and the fire is being increased by racial hatred. . . . It is urgent that this fever be stopped before the delirium causes irreparable harm."

Monseñor de Andrea was the founder and has been for many years the spiritual adviser of the Federation of Catholic Workers Associations, a women's trade union group in Buenos Aires. He strongly opposed the attempts by the government to gain control of the trade unions. In an interview with the author, he said that he was neither for nor against Perón, but that he *does* believe in certain principles—freedom of speech and press, democracy, trade union autonomy, Christianity, the Argentine Constitution—and when any of these things are subverted by whatever government, he will speak out in protest. In pursuance of his beliefs he preached sermons and published pamphlets in opposition to attempts by the Perón regime to suppress trade union autonomy and freedom of speech and press.

Monseñor de Andrea was for long one of the country's leading clergymen, and it had been supposed that when Argentina received a Cardinal's hat that it would go to him. However, when this great moment arrived, the honor was given not to Monseñor de Andrea but to his rival Bishop Copello. Copello was much more sympathetically inclined toward the Perón regime.

The long-run value for the Church of the kind of understanding which existed for some time between the hierarchy and Perón is a matter of considerable dispute. On the one hand, it is certainly true that among Perón's supporters the old anti-clerical feeling has virtually died. The author was told frequently in conversations with some of the older Peronista trade unionists that they did not particularly like the close link between Perón and the Church, but that it was not a sufficiently grave issue to get upset about, in view of the good things which Perón was doing.

Certainly the new trade unionists, brought into the labor movement during the Perón ascendancy, have little or none of the anti-clericalism which has historically been an important factor in the trade union movement of Argentina. In at least one instance, in the city of Mendoza, an important segment of the Peronista labor movement was actually organized under the direction and leadership of a Catholic priest.

On the other hand, the apparent agreement between the hierarchy and Perón aroused feelings of anti-clericalism in the opposition—feelings which had been virtually dead for decades. The Radical Party had to a large degree lost its anti-clerical tinge, but now includes the Church in its attacks against the regime. The Socialists, too, have reasserted their traditional anti-clerical sentiments. Their antagonism was particularly evident in the discussion of Catholic teachings in the government schools.

During President Perón's administration, relations between the Peronistas and the Argentine Church hierarchy have cooled noticeably. The first clash between the two came about over the question of legalizing prostitution. Until a few years ago there was a system of legally recognized and inspected houses of ill-fame. Through the influence of the Church this system was suppressed early in the 1940's and prostitution was completely outlawed.

President Perón and his wife sought to restore the system of legalized red light districts. This aroused the opposition of the Church officials, led by Cardinal Archbishop Copello, who publicly denounced the scheme in bitter terms. The Peróns, naturally, won the argument.

The next clash between Perón and the Church officialdom is graphically described by the February, 1951, issue of the magazine *Hemispherica:*

. . . the Papal Legate, arriving to preside at the National Eucharistic Congress in Rosario, discovered that Evita and Perón had purposely departed to their summer home in San Vicente, to avoid the need of greeting him.

In presenting his credentials to the Vice President, the Papal Legate diplomatically but forcefully pointed out the slight. During the entire Eucharistic Congress Perón failed to attend until the last day when, for political reasons, he found it best to hurry to the closing ceremony, and on his knees, pronounce a highly emotional discourse about brotherly love. The effect of this was completely obliterated a half hour later when, at a banquet tendered him by the chief of Rosario's police, he gave one of his most violent pronouncements against his political opponents, which certainly was intended to reach the ears of the gathered churchmen a few meters away.

With the evolution of the Peronista regime in the direction of totalitarianism, relations between Church and State in Argentina seem likely to become increasingly strained. Perón has not only reintroduced *Catholic* teaching in the state-supported schools, but he has introduced systematic *Peronista* propaganda among the schoolchildren. The teachers must devote a certain amount of time during the school day to a discussion of the life and teachings of Perón and their "significance" for the country. This is the frankest of political propaganda.

Furthermore, Perón has attempted to lift Peronismo from the status of a political doctrine to an article of faith for all Argentines; the implication being that what Perón and the Peronistas do is not to be questioned, not even by the Church. Of course, the situation is very different from that facing the Church in Eastern Europe, where the governments are headed by avowed atheists, for Perón and his wife are strongly Catholic in their religious beliefs. However, if the trend toward a totalitarian form of Peronismo continues, the teaching of that "one true faith of all Argentines" is likely to come into conflict with the teaching of the Faith of the Church.

PERONISMO AND CULTURE—
PERON AND THE
UNIVERSITIES

৪৹৪

THE MOST TENACIOUS ENEMIES of the Peronista regime have
been the intellectuals and professional classes. University students, in particular, were, from the beginning, in the forefront
of the struggle against the *de facto* regime and continued their
opposition after the inauguration of President-General Perón.

The students have played an active part in politics ever since
the First World War. Before that time the universities in
Argentina had been reactionary. The University of Córdoba,
dating back more than three hundred years, had been founded
by the Jesuits to train priests. The University of Buenos Aires
was founded by Rivadavia, one of the leaders of the revolt
against Spain, at the time of the War of Independence, but
had lost its liberal outlook during the dictatorship of Rosas
in the middle of the nineteenth century. The universities of
Santa Fe and Tucumán were provincial institutions, with a
provincial outlook. The only exception was the University of
La Plata, which was organized early in the twentieth century when liberal-minded Joaquin V. González was Minister
of Education.

The transformation of the universities started in Córdoba.

There the students went on strike early in 1918 in protest against the university administration. The strike had its rigorous moments. The students locked the Rector in a room and held him there for six days, refusing to allow him any food until he agreed to resign. Soon afterwards, President Irigoyen intervened and forced the adoption of a new regimen, in which the university was governed by representatives of the faculty and the student body.

During the 1920's this University Reform, as it became known throughout Latin America, spread to other universities. Tucumán and Santa Fe became national universities and adopted the new system of organization. The old faculties of theology, which had contributed greatly to the conservative outlook of the universities, were abolished, and the students became politically alert. By the time of the Revolution of 1943, five of the six universities were governed by their faculty and students, the only exception being the Universidad Nacional de Cuyo in Mendoza, which was a new institution, organized in 1936 by a Conservative educator and politician, Edmundo Correas. Correas was against the University Reform movement, had studied in the United States, and wanted to organize his university along American lines. As a result he went in heavily for social activities in the school, and forbade the organization of the kind of politically conscious student centers which existed in the other universities. He also allowed the Church to have considerable influence, particularly in the Faculty of Philosophy and Letters.

When the military seized control of the government in the June 4 Revolution, the students were not silent in their disapproval. Their fervent demonstrations against the new regime led the government to "intervene" the universities and place government appointees at their head.

At the Universidad del Litoral (the old University of Santa Fe), the interventor, Dr. Bruno Genta, who was reputed to

be a member of the anti-Semitic, pro-Nazi Alianza Liberta-
dora Nacionalista, expelled 380 of the 500 students in the
chemical engineering school; 580 of the 700 in the engineering school; and 1,028 of the 3,200 in the medical school.

For a few months there was comparative quiet. Then the
Manifesto for Democracy, protesting vigorously against the
measures of the regime, was signed in October, 1943, by leading figures of all walks of life. In retaliation many students
and professors (some three hundred of the latter) were
purged. The Minister of Education at this time was Martínez
Zuviría, who under the name of Hugo Wast had written violently anti-Semitic novels and pamphlets, which had been
widely circulated by the Nazis throughout Latin America.

With the wholesale firing of both teachers and students,
virtual warfare began between the students and the government and continued for about a year and a half. The government would not permit mention of the students' political
activities in the newspapers; the students were refused the
use of any printing presses and were forbidden to hold public
meetings. Most of the student leaders were jailed for longer
or shorter periods. Students were tortured, and in some cases
they responded with violence. One policeman in Rosario,
who was particularly active in torturing student prisoners,
was shot, gangster fashion, as he entered his front door one
evening. When President Farrell visited the University of
Buenos Aires to make a speech, a bomb was set off right under the platform from which he was to speak.

Early in 1945, temporary peace returned to the campuses
when all the ousted professors were restored to their posts
and the interventions were ended in the universities. There
is some indication that this change was made on the suggestion
of Colonel Perón, who perhaps hoped for student support for
his coming presidential campaign. It is true that late in 1944,
a delegation of students presented their grievances to Perón

and received assurances that all their wishes would be granted.

Conflict between the students and the regime broke out again late in September, 1945. Infuriated by the "March for the Constitution and Freedom," the government had renewed the state of siege (which had previously been lifted for a few weeks). Most of the important leaders of the opposition had been thrown into jail. The students decided to show their solid backing of the arrested leaders by an "occupation" of the universities, taking them over and refusing to leave. At the University of Buenos Aires students engaged in bloody clashes with the police and many were hospitalized, including a student who was the son of one of the Navy's leading admirals. This time, however, the Federal government did not intervene.

During the presidential campaign the students worked actively for the Tamborini-Mosca ticket, under the leadership of the Federación Universitaria Argentina, which since the University Reform in 1918 had been the main spokesman for the student body. Many of the student leaders were opposed to the joining forces of the Radical and Socialist parties with the Communists, since they had had trouble with the latter in the Federación Universitaria itself. However, once the decision to admit the Communists to the Unión Democrática was made, the students worked loyally and hard for the anti-Perón candidates.

Once Perón had won the presidency he took his revenge upon the universities. President Farrell once more decreed government intervention in all six on the claim that they had participated in politics. University autonomy has never been restored, at least on the basis on which it existed before the 1943 Revolution.

Determined to assure that the universities would no longer

be the seat of opposition to his regime, Perón undertook a university reform of his own. In the months following his accession to office, there was a thoroughgoing house-cleaning of the Argentine universities. In one week some two hundred teachers were discharged, and by the time the purge was over approximately two thousand people had been removed from the staffs of these institutions. Anyone who had given even a hint of opposition to the regime was gone. Included among those fired was Bernardo Houssay, who a few months later became the country's first Nobel Prize winner. Most of the professors have never been restored to their jobs, which were filled by "safe" Peronistas. The quality of instruction suffered considerably as a result of this drastic purge.

At the same time the government interventors removed all official recognition from the various student federations in the individual universities which together made up the Federación Universitaria.

President Perón publicly announced his intention of reorganizing the whole university system. He said he was going to do two things—put the university within the reach of all youth of the country who were capable and desirous of making use of its facilities, and reorganizing the whole teaching function.

His verbal onslaught on the old universities was violent. He declared:

Our universities merely served to give students a verbalist and hollow culture, without real depth, in which theory was not supplemented by practice, and even less by scientific investigation. Up to the present, our professionals and scientists have been obliged to teach themselves; they were formed, technically and scientifically, outside the halls of study.

The President attributed this sad state of affairs in part to the fact that professors neither lived with their students nor served as their guides and mentors. Generally, they devoted the main part of their time to private work, which was economically more profitable, and only taught as a sideline. The post of professor—it is sad to acknowledge—was, with honorable exceptions, merely a means to defray expenses, a degree to dazzle society, a bait to attract more private clientele.

In this last criticism Perón was not without reason. The procedure in virtually all Latin American universities is not to have a full-time teaching staff but to have a faculty consisting of people engaged full time in law, medicine, or one of the other professions, and who teach merely in their spare time. In the changes which Perón introduced in the university system he provided for the establishment of full-time teaching staffs.

The President made yet another charge against the universities, saying that "higher studies in our country . . . were out of reach for the humble. To enter a faculty it was necessary to enjoy certain economic standing, for two reasons: because studies were comparatively costly and because modest families need to increase their income with the work of their younger members, barely reaching fourteen years of age."

To this charge the anti-Peronistas replied that if the universities were not available to the poor man's son that was the fault of the government. One student leader pointed out that the appropriation for the universities in 1946 was about 33 million pesos, a large part of which went to support university hospitals, while the government was spending in that same year more than twelve times as much on the Federal Police and thirty times as much on the Army and Navy.

This student leader also added that in the Universidad del Litoral late in 1946 between 38 and 40 percent of the students were working their way through school, and all of these were sons of lower middle-class and working-class parents.

Nevertheless, Perón was on strong grounds when he recommended expanding the scholarship system to such an extent as to make it possible for any Argentine youth who desired to do so to go to a university. In June, 1949, all fees were abolished in the six national universities.

In outlining what kind of a university he hoped would result from his reforming efforts, President Perón said:

The University must also affirm and encourage a national and historical conscience; organize scientific investigation in such a manner as to encourage those who have vocation and capacity to undertake it; compile, organize and disseminate learning and culture; stimulate the progress of applied science and technical creation; form a teaching staff exclusively devoted to university scientific life; promote and establish free tuition; create and keep up research institutes; publish scientific works, and encourage the development of scientific, social, juridical, economic, literary and artistic studies and activities.

Despite the loftiness of these avowed aims, the Peronista reform of the universities undoubtedly had as its principal object the destruction of the centers of higher education as foci of anti-Perón student and faculty political activity. As a step in this direction, Perón changed the system of government of the universities, putting their administration in the hands of rectors appointed by the President of the Republic. Moreover, twenty of the twenty-five members of the Directing Committee of each university are appointed directly or indirectly by the President of the Republic. The universities are under the control of the Subsecretary of Culture, a new creation of the Peronista regime.

In addition to this, the selection of students was intended to be more "discreet" in the future. Since a large proportion of students receive scholarships granted by the national government, it may be supposed that a minimum of anti-Peronista applicants will be admitted; it may also be supposed that those who might develop anti-administration ideas would be careful not to express them too loudly for fear of losing their scholarships. To make doubly sure no trouble arises, the government announced at the beginning of the 1950 school year that each student must have a "certificate of good conduct" from the Federal Police before admission to classes.

To ensure closer control over all intellectuals, a Junta Nacional de Intelectuales was organized, with the avowed purpose to oversee all intellectual activities throughout the country, as well as to organize literary and artistic contests, cultural congresses, and the like.

Despite all these precautions, anti-Peronista activity among university students has not ceased. The Federación Universitaria, though now deprived of all official recognition, still exerts considerable influence. In mid-1950 it still claimed 10,000 members and the support of the majority of the student body. In 1949–1950 some of the leaders of the Federación were forced to seek refuge in Montevideo.

Even though considerable doubt thus remains concerning student loyalty toward Perón, it is evident that no such doubt exists in the case of the university administrations. Early in 1950 President Perón was given an honorary degree, on the same day, by all six of the national universities.

PERONISMO IN THE COUNTRYSIDE

෫෯෪

ARGENTINA remains an agricultural country. Despite the attempts of the Peronista regime to industrialize, the economy is still fundamentally agrarian. Hence, what the regime has done in the countryside is of utmost importance. Conditions in the rural areas of the country have long called for reform. Much of the richest agricultural land in Argentina has been for a hundred years the domain of the great landlords, or "hacendados," who have traditionally been the ruling class.

Although conditions of the rural workers and small landowners in Argentina have probably been better than in most of Latin America, they have been pitiable in many parts of the country. On the top of the agrarian heap have been the few thousand "hacendados," the "gran señores" who have held the destiny of the country in their hands. Beneath them, there have been some 150,000 small landowners, many of whom were owners of family farms, some of whom were employers of casual labor. At the bottom have been the 68 percent of the rural population of Argentina who have been virtual nomads, moving from one "chacra" or "hacienda" to another with the changing of the seasons.

The conditions of these rural workers varied a great deal from place to place. In provinces such as Santa Fe, where agricultural workers have been organized in unions since the

First World War, their lives were comparatively good. In the great "quebracho" and sugar plantations of northern Argentina, they were exceedingly poor; the workers were virtual slaves.

There the land was in the hands of great "colonization companies," whose ostensible object was to settle people on the land, but who actually sought to exploit the agricultural worker to the greatest possible degree.

Frequently the poor tenant who had spent years in building up the land which he rented from the "colonization company" found himself brutally thrown out of his small holding to make room for someone else who was willing to turn over still larger a proportion of the proceeds of his labor to the landowner. In such cases the law was always on the side of the landowner or colonization company, and, indeed, in many cases the landowner himself—or an employee of the colonization company—*was* the law. The companies or individual landowners often had their own private police to deal with recalcitrants and to see that no unauthorized person settled on their vast holdings.

Frequently landholdings ran to hundreds of thousands of hectares (a hectare is about two and a half acres), and some of the northern provinces and territories were owned by a few-score landlords. These were the real "oligarchy" of Argentina, and their holdings were huge. The Agricultural Census of 1937 showed that there were 452,007 farms, ranches, and haciendas in the country. Of these only 171,142 or 37.9 percent were worked by or for their owners. The percentage of farmer owners ranged from .2 percent in the Territory of Los Andes to 74.3 percent in the province of Tucumán. About two thirds of the corn and flaxseed farms were operated by nonowners, and the owners usually received 30–35 percent of the product.

Fifty-seven and a half percent of the farms (200,318) were

held by tenants, 39.4 percent by sharecroppers, and 2.5 percent were held on an arrangement combining fixed rent and sharecropping. About 55.4 percent of the tenants had no written contract, though this was contrary to the law.

Between 1914 and 1942 large landholdings in Buenos Aires province increased by about 5.4 percent of the total area, and at the end of this period about three hundred persons controlled one fifth of the land in the province. About half of the land was controlled by not more than 3,500 people. One professor in Buenos Aires University has said that in the early 1930's properties of 1,000 hectares (2,500 acres) or more comprised 68 percent, 67 percent, and 52 percent, respectively, of the total land in Buenos Aires, Santa Fe and Córdoba provinces. In Entre Ríos, properties of 2,000 hectares or over amounted to 40 percent of the land in the province.

One of the worst situations from the point of view of concentration of land ownership was found in the Territory of Misiones. This region had been sold by the province of Corrientes in 1881 and 29 people had bought some 2,101,026 of the territory's 2,918,000 hectares. By 1936 this territory was a center of yerba mate (a native tea) cultivation, concentrated in some 4,169 yerba mate farms. Of these, 94.5 percent were rated as small (having from one to 30,000 yerba mate plants) and 5.5 percent of the holdings were large (having from 30,000 to 1,000,000 plants). However, the small farmers had only 45.85 percent of the land, whereas the 231 large farmers owned 54.15 percent of the territory's acreage.

Previous to the 1943 Revolution comparatively little attention had been paid by politicians to the problem of agrarian reform. The Socialists had from time to time publicized the matter in Congress, and occasionally there were attempts to organize the workers in the sugar, tanning, or mate industries. However, these came to naught: the rural areas, and particularly the more backward among them, were the seat of the power of the Conservative oligarchy. The Conservatives remained in control of the national government because the rural landlords could "vote" their peons and tenants as they saw fit and could assure solid control of these backward provinces, which, though not large in population, nevertheless had senators and had votes in the electoral college which chose the Argentine president.

Cognizant of this situation, Perón, both before and after becoming president, appealed to the agricultural laborer, tenant, and sharecropper. During his election campaign he made a great deal of the promise to carry out a fundamental agrarian reform and to "give the land to the one who cultivates it."

Once in power, Perón began to put into execution a program which one supporter of the regime has described as consisting of the following three points:

1) With respect to the rural wage earner: establish a system similar to that of the city worker, guaranteeing him the same rights as the urban worker.

2) With respect to the rural entrepreneur: create a regime by which all will cultivate their own land, by making it easy for those who work the land to come to own it.

3) With respect to exploitation of the land: establish a system for selling the agricultural produce so as to assure the farmer decent prices and protect him against the risks of rural enterprise.

Three laws were passed to improve the position of the rural workers. The first of these is the so-called Statute of the Peon, which covers workers employed full time by individual farmers or agricultural corporations. The Statute of the Peon provides for a minimum wage, medical and pharmaceutical assistance, paid vacations, and indemnification for unjustified firing. It also establishes rules concerning one day of rest per week, food (if provided by the employer, it must meet health standards), and housing. The houses supplied by employers must have a certain minimum of air, natural light, and so on. Finally, the law provides for a system of voluntary savings, whereby the money which the worker wants to save can be deducted from his pay and placed by the employer in the Postal Savings Bank.

Prior to the passage of this law, the only reference to this type of agricultural worker in Argentine social legislation was a provision that wages be paid in Argentine money and that workers hurt while using agricultural machinery be included under workmen's compensation laws.

The second group of agricultural workers who were helped by the Perón administration were casual laborers employed only at harvest time. A law dealing especially with their case was passed in September, 1947; it established a National Commission of Rural Labor in the Ministry of Labor and Social Welfare. Regional commissions, composed of agricultural employers and workers and presided over by an official of the Ministry of Labor, were set up in each agricultural zone. These regional commissions agreed on the labor conditions to be observed in each region for the forthcoming harvest season. Such things as the length of the working day, the method of wage payment (whether by the hour or by piece work), the factors to be considered in setting the wage scale, the problem of "family labor," and the penalties to be imposed on workers or employers not carrying out the accord are covered in the decisions of the regional commissions. Any agreements between workers and employers which "modify or annul the rights and obligations" set up under the regional commissions' decisions are null and void. Three hundred and thirty such accords were made during the first year the law was in force.*

* Some light is thrown on the outlook of the Peronistas in the whole field of labor relations by the comment of a Peronista writer in the magazine *Hechos e Ideas,* who notes that "'With these commissions the procedure established by the Secretariat of Labor and Social Welfare for urban employment under

The third group covered by Peronista rural social legislation consisted of tenants and sharecroppers. Law No. 13,246, known as the Rent and Sharecropping Law, assures the renter or sharecropper of a tenure of at least eight years on the land he works. It provides that in case of a total loss of the crop through no fault of the renter the rent is to be forgiven; in case of partial loss, part of the rent is to be forgiven. As for sharecroppers, the share of the crop which must be paid to the landlord depends upon the proportion of the means of production which the two parties supply. The law further specifies that the landlord must provide a renter or share-cropper with a hygienic and healthful home. The landlord must contribute toward fighting blights and other hazards to the crop.

Finally, any improvements which the tenant makes in the land during his tenure must be recompensed by the land-lord when the tenant leaves. To assure that obedience to the law, regional committees composed of landlords and tenants and presided over by a representative of the Ministry of Agriculture were established.

The second major point in the Peronista agricultural pro-gram—and the one about which Perón and his friends have talked most, and done least—is giving land to the landless. Although Perón seems to have made considerably greater progress in this direction than his predecessors, his achieve-ments so far are a far cry from a thoroughgoing agrarian re-form.

Argentina has for many years had a modest program of "colonization," that is, settling landless workers on land of their own. Between 1940 and 1946 the Consejo Agrario

---

the leadership of the then Colonel Perón, were transferred to the country-side." This would seem to put the collective bargaining of urban unions and employers on the same footing as the decisions of avowedly government-con-trolled Regional Commissions of Rural Labor.

Nacional, which in this period had control of this program, had acquired some 260,672 hectares, but had actually distributed only 60,775 hectares, leaving 199,897 still in its hands after six years' operations. This colonization program was greatly accelerated after its management was transferred to the Banco de la Nación in 1946. Between July 1, 1946, and the end of December, 1949, the bank had acquired through expropriation and otherwise some 496,541 hectares and had turned over 305,230 hectares to settlers. Some 40,987 hectares were in the process of being transferred, leaving 150,414 still available.

This program has been dramatized by the Perón regime. For instance, one of the landholdings taken over by the government was that of Robustiano Patrón Costas, the candidate whom old President Castillo was pushing in the presidential election which was scheduled early in 1944 but never took place because of the June, 1943, *coup d'état*. Patrón Costas had come to be the archetype of the "oligarch," and to confiscate his land was to create the impression among the "peones" that a real attack was being made on the large landholding system.

This program of land reform has sometimes been a handy weapon against the opposition. For instance in September, 1949, the government moved to confiscate the "La Rosa" plantation in Salta. This was the property of Michel Torino, the director of the opposition paper *El Intransigente*.

If Perón were to carry out a thoroughgoing agrarian reform, he would perhaps unwittingly lay the economic basis for the political democracy which he had been busy destroying. The large landholding system has always been a hindrance to the development of a true democracy in Argentina, and the establishment of a strong class of small farmers cultivating their own land might go far toward making such a democracy possible. As yet, however, there is little indication that Perón has any intention of carrying out such a full-blown agrarian reform.

Perhaps the feature of the Peronista agricultural program most attacked by the Opposition has been the government monopoly of the purchase and sale of agricultural products. In 1946 the government established the Instituto Argentino de Producción e Intercambio (Argentine Institute of Production and Exchange), more commonly known by its initials as the I.A.P.I. The Institute was first given the right to purchase the whole of the nation's wheat crop, and later it came to have a monopoly on the purchase of all major crops. The Institute also was commissioned to sell these crops wherever the best price could be found. Finally, the I.A.P.I. was empowered to undertake the purchase of necessary machinery and materials for the nation's agricultural production, and for some time virtually had a monopoly in this field.

The reason given for establishing this government monopoly was the desire to avoid a repetition of the sad situation which occurred after the First World War, when the entire wheat crop was bought at ruinous prices (for the Argentine farmer) by a Commission organized in the Allied countries. The Argentine government decided in 1945 that, if there was going to be a "single buyer" (the Allies) after the Second World War, there should also be a "single seller" (the Argentine government), and for that purpose it organized the I.A.P.I.

Several serious charges have been made against the I.A.P.I. by opponents of the Perón regime. First of all, opposition leaders argue that the government is exploiting the farmers of Argentina a great deal more than foreigners ever did. They point out that in March, 1946, wheat was selling at 18.20 pesos a hundred kilos, with indications that prices would go up still further.

However, in April the government took over the purchase of all the country's wheat and decided to pay only 15 pesos per 100 kilos. *La Prensa* quoted the London *Daily Telegraph* as saying that the Argentine government thus made 7,500,000 pounds sterling on an operation involving the sale of 15 million pounds sterling worth of wheat. The government at this time was reported as buying linseed at 35 pesos per kilo and selling it at 90–100 pesos. The same thing was occurring with the corn crop, on which the government was reported to have made some 700 million pesos in 1946–1947. In the next year, as prices continued to rise, the profits of the government were even greater.

Peronista spokesmen, including the President himself, have admitted that the government has made very large paper profits on the purchase and sale of the country's agricultural goods. Peronista Senator Duran, speaking in the presence of the President, did not hesitate to say that the I.A.P.I. was buying wheat for twenty pesos a quintal and selling it for sixty. However, he and all the other Peronista spokesmen pleaded extenuating circumstances.

The first public accounting of the activities of I.A.P.I., in mid-1948, was described by the London *Economist* as "not as informative as it might be." However, the report did reveal that the I.A.P.I. had an outstanding debt of over three billion pesos, most of which was owed to government banks. It showed that the Instituto had made a profit of two billion pesos in the twelve months preceding the report, and held as its chief assets one and a third billion pesos' worth of government securities.

The second argument which the opposition raises against the operations of the I.A.P.I. is that as a result of the unreasonably low prices which the farmers are getting for their products, in contrast to the high world-market rates, there is a growing tendency among the farmers to migrate to the cities and to abandon production of agricultural goods. *La Vanguardia* in May, 1949, published figures indicating that in less than ten years the area sown in wheat had declined by about two million hectares, in linseed by about a million, and in corn by about four million hectares. The writer roundly criticized the government's program, saying that the decline in production was due "not only to the lack of machinery but to the fact that the prices offered by the government for the agricultural products do not compensate for the work put into growing the produce nor cover the costs of production."

Perón himself gives somewhat oblique support to this argument in an article on "The Economic Reform" in which he notes that although the United States was exporting 1,200 quintales of grain in 1947 for every 100 shipped per year during 1934–1938, Argentina was shipping only 30 in 1947 for every 100 shipped each year during the 1934–1938 period.

In April, 1950, the government, undoubtedly alarmed by the decrease in farm production, finally decided to give the farmers a sizable rise in prices. The administration announced that farmers would receive 20 percent more for the 1950 crop than they had received in the previous year, and at the same time called for the planting of 25 percent more acreage in wheat and 50 percent more in corn.

In the third place, the opposition charged that the I.A.P.I. was shot through with graft and corruption. One incriminating story, which *La Vanguardia* told at length, concerned some 997 jeeps, apparently United States war surplus, which the I.A.P.I. bought from an unnamed friend of the regime, who himself is said to have gotten them for $225 apiece in the United States. The jeeps were purchased from him for $1,200 dollars apiece and about that much more was spent to get them into condition.

La Vanguardia claimed that I.A.P.I. spent some thirty million pesos to buy radios for families of government officials;

that it bought 5,000 tractors at a price equivalent to an index number of 100, when they could have been purchased on the open market for 25, and that I.A.P.I. thus spent 20 million pesos more than these tractors were worth. *La Vanguardia* also alleged that many of the tractors were found to be unserviceable and were sold by I.A.P.I. for only 5,750 pesos each, though they cost 8,200 pesos apiece.

That some of these graft charges are probably true is indicated by the fact that Miguel Miranda, chief of I.A.P.I. for over two years, virtually admitted that there was something wrong with the "jeep" deal. Moreover, the rough treatment given those members of the opposition who have attacked the I.A.P.I. hints that their statements are not far-fetched.

A few weeks after Perón's inauguration, Radical Deputy Rodriguez Araya made charges that there had been corruption in the granting of export licenses to Uruguay. In September, 1946, Rodriguez Araya was shot and seriously wounded in his home city of Rosario, by three policemen dressed in plain clothes. He later was expelled from the Chamber of Deputies by the Peronista majority in that body and was forced to take refuge in Montevideo.

In Uruguay he divulged other extravagances of I.A.P.I. He told of the importation of rayon from Italy in July, 1948; only bona fide textile manufacturers were supposed to receive licenses to import this rayon. However, Rodriguez Araya says that only Silvio Tercerri, a friend (and agent?) of Miranda was granted actual permission to import. Tercerri was not even a manufacturer, but all textile factories had to buy from him.

Miranda himself was finally ousted as head of I.A.P.I. because of a scandal concerning one of his operations. Acting as head of the I.A.P.I., Miranda is claimed by Rodriguez Araya to have closed a deal for the import of 120 million pesos' worth of textiles from Brazil. Before the deal was finally closed Miranda is said to have demanded and received a 16⅔ percent commission on the deal. The purchase was never consummated, but Miranda had his twenty million. However, he was out as head of I.A.P.I., after the matter was brought to Perón's attention.

The President and his friends have probably spent more time defending the policies of the I.A.P.I. in speeches, articles and press conferences, than any other phase of the government's program. Perón has argued that the I.A.P.I. operations have been beneficial for the Argentine farmer, evoking as proof the fact that the Argentine agriculturalists received eight to ten times as much for their products in 1947 as in 1918.

Perón and others have made much of the fact that the sales of these agricultural products by the Peronista government have not been for cash, but rather that most of them have been in the form of barter deals with other countries. Therefore, they argue, the monetary value placed on Argentine wheat, linseed, corn, and other products is only nominal, since no money has ever been involved—Argentina receiving necessary imports in return for I.A.P.I's exports.

The government spokesmen also declare that the profits made by the government have been widely used to subsidize foodstuffs within Argentina, and in other ways to keep down the cost of living in the country. In the process of these operations, the government lost 400 million pesos in the first two years of I.A.P.I., according to an interview President Perón gave in February, 1948.

The President and his supporters lay considerable stress on the contribution which I.A.P.I. made in obtaining necessary agricultural machinery immediately after the war. By being able to buy in large orders and to scour the whole earth for the needed implements, the I.A.P.I. could get them when private buyers probably could not have done so. Miguel

Miranda told a press conference that the purchase of trucks by I.A.P.I. had resulted in Argentine exports rising from 400,000 tons to 1,200,000 tons. These trucks were bought by I.A.P.I. and sold to private truckers on long-term credit. Some 50 million pesos were spent on this operation. Agricultural implements, jeeps, and other machinery were also purchased by the Institute.

In view of the comparatively small amount of reliable information on the actual functioning and the finances of I.A.P.I. it is somewhat difficult to give a final assessment of the operation of that government monopoly. It is certainly true that the Argentine government has been able to do a lot of things which it could not otherwise have done as a result of the operations of this agency.

The full record will perhaps never be known, but it seems likely that a good deal of the industrialization and militarization programs of the Perón government have been financed through the I.A.P.I. The Institute has provided foreign exchange which could then be used however the Perón government saw fit, with no need to report to Congress on how the funds have been spent, or to ask Congress for the money in the first place. Perhaps the most important feature of I.A.P.I.'s operations is just that—that it has provided the Perón regime with a great deal of money—albeit in foreign exchange which could only be materialized by the importation of foreign commodities—for which it did not have to account.

Thus one of the underlying foundations of any democratic representative regime—that the elected legislature have the final say on finances—has been seriously weakened through the medium of the Instituto Argentino de Producción e Intercambio.

ARGENTINA FOR THE ARGENTINES—PERON'S ECONOMIC PROGRAM

❧

JUAN DOMINGO PERÓN never misses a chance to pat himself on the back. In a dramatic gesture on July 9, 1947, the President led his followers in swearing allegiance to a Declaration of Economic Independence in the city of Tucumán, in the very house in which the country's political independence had been proclaimed in the year 1816. Thus Argentina's master showman deftly directed public attention and praise to his much-propagandized program to achieve the vaunted "Economic Independence of Argentina."

Perón has sought to acquire this "economic independence" through several policies. First of all, he has tried to put under Argentine ownership the chief foreign-owned industries in the country and to repatriate the nation's foreign debt. In the second place, he has sought to diminish the excessive dependence of the country's economy on the export of agricultural products through a program of industrialization.

In part as a result of these policies, Perón has been faced with another pressing economic problem—inflation. The steady increase of prices, at first denied and then admitted with explanations, has plagued Perón since he became President. The measures taken to combat inflation have therefore formed the third principal feature of the economic program of the Perón regime.

President Perón seized the occasion of the fourth anniversary of October 17 to delineate the chief achievements in his campaign for "economic independence." He said:

We have nationalized the Central Bank and insurance.

We have bought the railroads and their 17,000 adjoining properties.

We have bought the telephones and all means of transmission.

We have bought the public services of gas, energy, transport, running water etc.

We have bought the ports and the grain elevators.

We have nationalized the sale of the country's agricultural production.

We have paid the foreign debt, which was costing two and a half million pesos a day, for each Argentine.

We have created a merchant fleet which is one of the world's most important.

We have reequipped our industry, our transport and our ports.

In less than three years we have bought all of these things worth more than ten billion pesos, and have not only paid for them in cash, but have passed from being a debtor state to being one of the world's few creditor nations. . . .

We have acquired all of these, but we have acquired much more—our independence, our dignity, our pride.

The Perón regime has clearly indicated that the regime has no qualms about government participation in economic affairs. Not only has it nationalized many of the country's basic industries, but it has also carried out a large program of government-directed economic development, and has set up several institutions for the purpose of exercising general supervision over the economy. The first such institution was the National Postwar Council, established by Vice President Perón in 1944. Its purpose was the planning of postwar economic developments and its chief accomplishment was the elaboration of the Five Year Plan.

The National Postwar Council was succeeded by the National Economic Council, whose first chief was Miguel Miranda. The Council's duties included the supervision of the Five Year Plan as well as the fight against inflation. Its head was for a time virtual "economic czar" of Argentina. In 1949, after Miranda fell from favor, a National Council of Economic Cooperation was set up to advise the National Economic Council. Among its members were representatives of the country's principal economic groups, including agriculture, grazing, commerce, industry, importers, rural workers, industrial workers, white collar workers, consumers, and two representatives of the C.G.T. The wide scope of the National Economic Council and its advisory body is evident from the fact that the latter itself set up four subcommittees to cover the fields in which its advice would be likely to be sought: a) development of production; b) development of exchange; c) commercial organization; d) development of housing and construction in general.

Fundamental to the Perón economic program was the desire to loosen foreign control over many of the nation's key industries. In most cases the "Argentinized" industries were taken over by the government. The first important institution to be nationalized was the Central Bank, which had been controlled by a board of directors made up largely of representatives of the big foreign banks operating in Argentina. (President Perón sometime later claimed that only four members of this board spoke Spanish.) On March 25, 1946, even before the inauguration of Perón as president, his predecessor, General Farrell, issued a decree nationalizing the Banco Central and appointing Miguel Miranda as its first president.

The reorganized bank was given extensive powers. In addition to its regular function as a central bank, it was given control over all other banks, and over all bank deposits. It was empowered to withhold loans from any person or institution, and to seize bank accounts if necessary. The government thus assumed control of all the country's financial resources.

The second step in the nationalization campaign was the purchase of the nation's telephone system, the United River Platte Telephone Company, a subsidiary of the American-owned International Telephone and Telegraph Company. In September, 1946, President Perón announced that he had negotiated the purchase of the system for $94,991,364, a very generous sum. The government was taken vigorously to task by the opposition for talking strenuously against "Yankee Imperialism" on the one hand and making deals very much to the "Yankee Imperialists'" advantage.

The nationalization of the railroads was not as simple a job as the taking over of the Central Bank and the telephones. Early in 1947 an agreement was reached for the purchase of the British-owned roads, which made up most of the Argentine railroad network, for a price of 150,000,000 pounds sterling. Although at the time it was announced that the roads would be transferred in the near future, over a year passed before the final details of the arrangement had been consummated.

The purchase of the railroads was tied up with the renegotiation of the Anglo-Argentine meat and wheat agreement, and a general accord on these matters could not be reached until February, 1948. The treaty—the so-called Andes Agreement—provided that Argentina send food worth 190 million pounds sterling to Great Britain in exchange for the railroads and some 40 million pounds' worth of machinery, coal, and oil. British railway stock and bondholders were to be paid from Argentine credits resulting from the exports to Great Britain during the year 1948–1949, with the British government advancing 100 million pounds.

The British-owned lines thus acquired by the Argentine government were the Argentine Great Southern, the Buenos Aires Pacific, and the Western Railway; altogether, these covered some 27,000 miles of track. They had been built by the British at the end of the nineteenth century and were being operated under a 99-year franchise. The equipment, stations, and other features of the railroads were patterned on those in Britain, and in many cases were imported from the United Kingdom. Anyone used to riding on the British railroads would feel quite at home on those of Argentina.

During the year in which negotiations were in process the lines were allowed to deteriorate very seriously, since the British owners had no particular interest in investing more money in them, and the Argentine government naturally chose to hold back repairs until it acquired control.

However, immediately after the roads became the property of the Argentine government, a large reequipment and repair program was begun. In June, 1948, thirty Baldwin steam locomotives were shipped to Argentina from the United States, and orders were placed for seventy-five engines to be constructed by the Cooper-Bessemer Corporation. A number of electric locomotives were ordered from General Electric, while over one hundred freight cars were contracted for in the United States. The railways also purchased 65 Diesel-electric locomotives, built in the United States on designs made by Argentine engineers; 414 flatcars made in Canada, and rails and fish plates imported from Great Britain.

Another major step in Perón's program for achieving "economic independence" was the repurchase of the Argentine foreign debt, much of which was held in London. Much of the blocked sterling which Argentina had in London after the war and which could not be used immediately to purchase needed products was used for this purpose. In August, 1947, Perón was in a position to state that "Argentina . . .

has no foreign debt, since it has all been cancelled, making us one of the world's three creditor countries." Argentina had had a foreign debt of some 12,500,000,000 pesos.

The Perón government has been very cautious about contracting any new foreign debt. When a loan of $125,000,000 was negotiated with the Export-Import Bank of Washington, D.C., in May, 1950, a group of private banks actually received the grant, while the Argentine government merely guaranteed the loan. Strictly speaking, Perón could then still say that Argentina had no foreign debt.

A very important feature of the economic program has been the emphasis on development projects. The over-all program of economic development was first put forward in the Five Year Plan which President Perón presented to Congress for approval in October, 1946. This Five Year Plan, as then presented was in essence the whole catalogue of reforms which the Peronista government hoped to accomplish during its term in office. The Plan included such political items as the granting of the right to vote to women, the reorganization of the universities, as well as the economic features.

The purpose of the economic sections of the Plan was to step up the industrialization of the country, with particular attention to the creation of new sources of energy and power. It was proposed to carry out investments of 5,965 million pesos, at that time equivalent to $1,500 million, with the largest single category of investment, some 2,235 million pesos, to be in power projects of various kinds.

Other parts of the Plan foresaw expenditures on public works and transportation facilities, immigration and colonization, public health and the development of new productive resources—fisheries, agricultural experimentation, research, and manufacturing industries.

In presenting the Five Year Plan to Congress, Perón announced that it would give work to 83,650 Argentines and would make possible the entry into Argentina of about 250,000 immigrants.

In addition to direct government investment through administrative departments, government-owned corporations and mixed corporations, the Plan provided for legislation giving exemption and preferential customs treatment to those establishing new industries.

To manage one of its most important projects—the development of new sources of power and energy—a Dirección General de Energia was established. Under this were set up four subsidiary bureaus dealing with petroleum, solid mineral fuels, vegetable fuels and derivatives, and water and electric energy.

In the field of electric energy the government claimed late in 1949 that the installed power had risen from 29,906 kilowatts in 1946 to 53,634 in 1947 and 81,120 in 1948. Some 243,280,000 kilowatt hours were generated in 1948, and the number of users had increased to 153,300. According to the Plan some thirty-five construction projects costing a total of 606,400,000 pesos, should have been started in this field during 1947. But in fact, 45 were begun, totaling 851,800,000 pesos. In 1949 the works under construction or about to begin totaled 1,118,056,400 pesos; and those studied and projected called for the expenditure of 979,730,000. Installed power amounted to 159,507 kilowatts in 1949, and when the projects then under construction were finished, would amount to 594,850 kilowatts. Production in 1949 was 711,200,000 kilowatt hours and when the projects then under construction were completed the system could produce 2,084,400,000 kilowatt-hours (equivalent to 1,397,800 tons of coal).

With regard to natural gas, the Plan proposed to build three pipe lines. Two of these were completed by the latter part of 1949 and the government claimed that the additional amount of gas thus made available had resulted in reducing the price from 0.2993 pesos a cubic meter of 4,500 calories in March, 1945, to 0.2694 per cubic meter in 1949. It was estimated that the completion of all these gasoducts would quadruple the supply of gas available in Buenos Aires.

One important aspect of the energy and power section of the Five Year Plan was the program for reforestation. Wood has been an important source of fuel and energy in Argentina, particularly during the Second World War. Before that conflict, Argentina imported about 45 percent of the combustible material she used, but during the 1943–1945 period she imported only 7 percent. Much of the difference was made up by the uneconomic use of wood. Under the Plan it is proposed to restore some of this loss, and at the same time to develop still further the use of wood for fuel and power.

Of great help to the development program of the Peronista administration has been the Banco de Crédito Industrial Argentino, which was established by the revolutionary regime in 1944. The bank has aided the development of industries in two ways—by making loans, and by investing directly in enterprises. It has been particularly active in financing the expansion of the country's merchant marine, its fishing industry, and its mining industry. It has given special aid to small miners in need of additional capital.

In 1947 the Banco de Crédito Industrial made loans totaling 56,000,000 pesos, and in 1946, 116,000,000 pesos. About three quarters of these loans went to companies in the Buenos Aires metropolitan area, though there is an increasing tendency to extend aid to provincial industries.

The exact extent of the growth of manufacturing in Argentina is not known. Perón maintained that industry increased 500 percent from 1943–1947, "and now boasts an iron and steel industry, coal mines and various other raw materials; makes all the powder and explosives needed in the country and makes all its arms, munitions and vehicles."

These claims are an exaggeration of the achievements of the Perón regime. However, the iron and steel industry is definitely an accomplishment of the General's government. The new steel industry turned out its first ingots in 1945. A steel plant was set up in Palpala, under military control. By 1950 Argentina was producing 150,000 tons of semifinished steel a year and the government was planning the establishing of new facilities capable of producing between 800,000 and a million tons a year.

Considerable progress has undoubtedly been made in the field of transportation. Both on the sea and in the air, Argentine flagships have increased in number with great rapidity. Before the Second World War the merchant marine was a small one. It got a considerable boost when the government took over all Axis ships interned in the country, but it was not until the inauguration of Perón that its expansion was undertaken in earnest.

It was announced early in 1950 that the Argentine merchant fleet, built and building, included 1,364,000 tons, as opposed to 233,700 tons in 1943. By 1953 the Argentine merchant marine is scheduled to be the world's third largest. Most of the country's new ships have been built with an eye to speed, and make from seventeen to twenty knots an hour. The new vessels include three luxury passenger liners of 14,500 tons: the *Presidente Perón,* the *Eva Duarte de Perón* and the *17 de Octubre.* There were in March, 1950, some forty motor ships on order for Argentina in British and continental yards, totaling 275,000 tons, and new ships were arriving in Buenos Aires virtually every week.

The government began to take an active interest in reorganizing the civil aviation industry in 1945. A decree of April 27 of that year provided that "the airlines, as well as any other commercial aviation activity, operating domestically preferably shall be undertaken by the State itself or by mixed capital companies." A subsequent decree provided that the Lineas Aereas del Estado (LADE), which is operated by the Air Ministry, was to have the job of overseeing the entire civil aviation industry.

Subsequently Argentine civil aviation was reorganized into five companies, with the Flota Aerea Mercante Argentina (FAMA) operating the international routes, and four other companies, including Lineas Aereas del Estado, operating the domestic ones. All these companies are at least partly government owned: the government has a one-third interest in FAMA, owns LADE completely, and has a 20 percent interest in the others. In all cases the president and vice president, as well as a varying proportion of the other members of the boards of directors, are appointed by the government.

After 1946 there was a considerable expansion of Argentine civil aviation, particularly notable in the case of FAMA. Starting with connections with neighboring capitals, FAMA in 1946 inaugurated its first European run, to London via Lisbon and Paris. Subsequently two European flights were set up, one to Madrid and thence to Paris and London, another to Madrid and on to Rome. Other routes operated by FAMA in America go to Rio de Janeiro and on to Havana, Cuba; and to Santiago, Chile.

The extensive economic development program of the Perón administration has undoubtedly stimulated and augmented the inflation which plagues Argentina today. There are several other causes for this rise in prices. The international inflationary trend, which continued until late 1948 and has been resumed since the outbreak of the Korean war, has resulted in a steady increase in prices of goods imported into Argentina from inflation-hit countries.

Of some importance, too, is the decline in labor productivity since the beginning of the *de facto* regime in 1943. Perón himself admitted in 1948 that labor productivity had fallen from a level of 100 in 1943 to 89.2. The Perón government has never been unaware of or indifferent to the problem. No sooner was the General inaugurated than he began a widely ballyhooed, but generally ineffectual "battle of sixty days." The "battle" was in essence an attempt to convince Argentine businessmen that they should not raise prices and at the same time to persuade the workers that prices were not being raised.

Subsequently various approaches to the problem were tried. The powers of the Central Bank were utilized, and in July, 1947, the Bank announced a restriction on credit for speculative ventures. Nevertheless, bank loans increased from the end of 1946 to the middle of 1948 from 5,400 million pesos to 13,600 million pesos, and during the same period rediscounts by the Central Bank rose from 3,720 million to nearly 12 billion.

In October, 1948, the tightening of credit and currency controls was announced by the National Economic Council, which had taken over the direction of the anti-inflation campaign. That drastic measures were then necessary is indicated by the fact that Central Bank note circulation had increased from 2,830 million pesos in December, 1945, to 6,660 millions in October, 1948.

One of the principal methods used by the *de facto* and Perón administrations in their anti-inflation efforts was the subsidization of foodstuffs. Figures on this activity are hard to come by, but Perón, in defending the operations of I.A.P.I., did reveal that the government was buying wheat at twenty pesos from the farmer, and selling it to the miller at nine pesos a quintal, thus making it possible for bread to sell at 35–45 centavos a kilo. (Later bread went to a peso a kilo.)

La Vanguardia noted in August, 1949, that the government was subsidizing the meat supply of the Federal capital to the tune of 72 million pesos a year, by paying 40 centavos for each kilo sold there. The same issue said that some 46 million pesos a year was being spent to subsidize cooking oils, 79 millions to subsidize seed oils, 15 million pesos to subsidize the pasteurized milk supply of Buenos Aires. It estimated that these food subsidies had amounted to about 210 million pesos a year, but that they had recently been suppressed. Subsidization of the sugar industry to the amount of 250–300 million pesos a year and of bread to about 300 million pesos a year still continued.

The food industries were not the only ones so subsidized. The electrical industry was said by the same issue of *La Vanguardia* to have received 36 million pesos from the government to cover a wage increase, and the cement industry was said to collect 80 centavos in subsidy for each bag of cement manufactured and sold.

More drastic steps were also taken against inflation. In June, 1947, the government instituted a program of fixing retail prices and seized factory stocks of clothing and shoes for distribution at these prices. Numerous price violators were arrested. Early in 1948 the release from prison of seventy of these violators was announced, though the statement gave no indication as to how long they had been jailed. Later that year four United States citizens were penalized for price violations.

One of the difficulties of this approach was that the government itself changed the "maximum" prices, usually in an upward direction. Thus *La Vanguardia* on February 1, 1949, pointed out that in 1948, when the legal price for Coca Cola was fifty centavos, and for a glass of beer 1.50 pesos, numerous people had gone to jail for violating the fixed prices; but that in January, 1949, the price of a "coke" was raised by the government to 90 centavos and of a beer to three pesos.

Another strategy was to suppress the figures on wages and living costs. Even as early as late 1946 the publication of this data was months behind, and the situation grew worse rather than better later on.

When all other methods failed, Perón and his associates fell back on persuasion. They developed a propaganda campaign to convince the people that their inflation was a "good" one, as compared with disastrous ones in other countries. In a speech in March, 1949, Perón characterized the Argentine inflation as an "inflation of riches" resulting from the growing wealth of the country. He proclaimed that consumption of goods had increased by 350 percent since 1943. Finally, he claimed that, in any case Argentine prices were 20 percent below world prices.

Previously, Miguel Miranda, then "economic dictator" of the country, commented on Argentine inflation thus:

I ask, inflation of what? Our inflation is very different from the other kind; it does not arise from the emission of currency, because there is production. There are many economists who say that there is a great deal of money in the hands of the people. It could be; but, before, the people didn't even have five centavos and now they have pesos in their pockets. And that is not inflation. I ask these economists if Argentina could get along with less money. It could not, because the circulating medium has to be in accord with production. I think, therefore, that all of this inflation talk is out of date, or is malicious.

Be it out of date or malicious or whatever else, the "inflation talk" dealt with real facts. A correspondent of the London *Economist* wrote in the April 9, 1949, issue of that magazine:

It is unfortunate that no reliable cost of living indices are available. Official figures, based on 1939 as 100, give the index at the end of 1948 at 190; but to anyone living in Argentina since 1939 this figure is patently absurd. To put it in the neighborhood of 300 would be no exaggeration, and perhaps 400 is nearer the mark.

In reply to Señor Miranda's talk of the rising price level as an "inflation of wealth," this same correspondent pointed out that between 1946 and 1947 Argentina's national income rose only from 5,038 million pesos to 5,404 million, about 7 percent, and that even some of this increase was illusory.

Some further doubt is cast upon the Peronista claims by Argentine government sources themselves. Perón's claim of an increase of 350 percent in the consumption of goods is put in a somewhat peculiar light by the announcement of the Central Bank in June, 1948 that national production had risen 7 percent during 1947. Even if the rate had been 7 percent during all the years of the *de facto* government, that would only amount to a total increase of slightly more than 30 percent for the four and a half years from 1943 to 1947. And there is more than a little doubt that production increases were at the same rate in the years 1943–1946.

In spite of all Peronista propaganda to the contrary, the inflation is real enough. In 1949 all public services, including the railroads, increased their prices. The costs of other commodities also increased significantly. Gasoline soared from 35 centavos to 60 centavos a litre. Bread increased from 50 centavos a loaf to 80; meat rose from one peso eighty centavos to two pesos fifty centavos. Clothing prices also soared.

The causes of inflation were various. Aside from those already mentioned, the government's economic development program, and the world-wide inflation, some of the blame can be attributed to the government itself. Undoubtedly the unproductive nature of much of the expenditure of the Perón government—building barracks, buying military equipment, and the like—is a factor. So, too, is the shortage of dollars, which has been a grave problem since 1948. It came about through reckless spending by the government, which exhausted the sizable reserve of gold and dollars accumulated during the Second World War. Lacking dollars, the things which Argentina would naturally import from the United States and other dollar countries are in short supply, and hence have a tendency to go up in price.

The increase in currency during the Perón Era has been another important cause of inflation. In 1943 the circulating medium was 2,131,000,000 pesos, and by the first half of 1949 it had risen to 8,000,000,000 pesos.

Finally, it is probably true that the labor policies of the government spurred the upswing of the inflationary spiral. Having gained his original popularity in part by decreeing wage increases for all worker groups who demanded them during his tenure as Secretary of Labor, Perón has found it very difficult to shut off this source of the good things of life. That he has tried to do so is indicated by the growing number of strikes that have been staged by Peronista unions and have been declared illegal by the government. However, that he has not been entirely successful was demonstrated in the Tucumán sugar workers' strike of 1949, when Perón decreed an end to the walkout but at the same time granted the workers a 60 percent wage increase.

These wage boosts do not help the situation. A large part of the country's industrial effort is concentrated on the production of capital goods and military equipment and supplies, and the dollar shortage is causing increasing difficulty in importing the manufactured goods needed by a nation still essentially agricultural. Higher wages thus put a very serious pressure on the supply of consumer goods available and help to push up prices on these goods.

On the other hand, one should not pass over without comment the claims of the Peronistas that the standard of living of the average Argentine has been increasing since 1943. This is probably true. Argentina was in an extremely fortunate position during the last year or so of the war and in the immediate postwar period, in that her agricultural products were in very great demand throughout the world, and she could virtually name her own price. In return for some of the dollars and pounds received for these exports, Argentina imported some of the goods which her people needed.

Furthermore, the home consumption of agricultural products has undoubtedly increased a good deal since before the Second World War. Peronista economist Carlos Alberto Emery in an article in the magazine *Hechos e Ideas* claimed that in 1948 some 6,764,000 head of cattle were slaughtered for home consumption, an increase of 35 percent over the 1943–1947 annual average of 5,013,000. He noted that the production of butter—most of which is consumed at home—had increased from 22,500 tons in 1938 to 36,000 tons in 1948; and that the production of cheese had gone up from 35,000 tons in 1939 to 74,000 in 1948.

Inflation remains a serious problem in Argentina. It is a problem which might in the long run unseat the government, since continued inflation might turn the great mass of labor against Perón. And it is labor's support that permits General Perón to remain El Presidente.

ARGENTINA'S PLACE IN THE SUN—PERON'S FOREIGN POLICY

৪৩

THERE IS A STRIKING contrast in the international status of Argentina at the time of the inauguration of Juan Domingo Perón as President of the Republic and her status two or three years later. In that period and under the General's administration, the Platine Republic was able to recoup all the diplomatic losses sustained under the Castillo and the *de facto* government. It achieved a position of power and prestige scarcely equaled in the nation's history.

Perón himself called attention to this in a speech to the Peronista members of Congress delivered in the Casa Rosada (the Argentine White House) on February 5, 1948. He contrasted various aspects of the country's international position prior to his inauguration on June 4, 1946, with the situation at the time of his speech:

a. *Before June 4, 1946:* Insufficient relations with the American countries.
 At the present time: Relations consolidated with all the American peoples.
b. *Before June 4, 1946:* Lack of solidarity and comprehension by the European states and other countries throughout the world.

At the present time: Rebirth of cordiality and cooperation with the European countries.

c. *Before June 4, 1946:* Lack of relations with the Soviet Union, a nation whose importance in political affairs needs no demonstration.

   At the present time: Establishment of diplomatic relations with the Soviet Union.

d. *Before June 4, 1946:* Lack of any influence in international assemblies, which Argentina did not attend and to which she was not invited.

   At the present time: Recovery of prestige in world assemblies, with Argentina's word having new weight.

e. *Before June 4, 1946:* Positions of authority in international organizations completely closed to Argentina.

   At the present time: Member of Security Council of the United Nations; member of the United Nations Emergency Fund; member of the most important commissions of the United Nations Assembly.

f. *Before June 4, 1946:* Difficulties in commercial intercourse.

   At the present time: Commercial intercourse with all the peoples of the world and the opening of all ports to Argentine products.

g. *Before June 4, 1946:* Difficulties for the projection of our culture.

   At the present time: Expansion of Argentine culture throughout the universe.

There is more than a little truth in this boastful demonstration of the diplomatic achievements of the Perón administration. When the General was inaugurated, about the only European country with which Argentina had friendly relations was Spain; in the Western Hemisphere her relations with the United States were exceedingly bad and those with most of the other American countries were not much better.

In subsequent years, Perón maintained his friendly relations with Spain. Asked a year or so after taking office why it was that he maintained such close contacts with the Caudillo regime, Perón is reported to have replied that Franco was the only foreign ruler to stick by Argentina in its hour of need, and so he intended to stick with Franco. He did so, in the United Nations and outside of it, until 1949. Within the United Nations, Argentina led the forces opposed to the international boycott of the Generalissimo's regime. Argentina refused to abide by the decision of the United Nations to recall Ambassadors from Madrid. The Argentine Ambassador remained in the Spanish capital throughout the period of the United Nations quarantine.

In the economic sphere the help which Perón gave to Franco was even more tangible. Several large loans were made, to be spent on the purchase of Argentine cattle and wheat for consumption in poverty-stricken and still war-wracked Spain. Franco publicized this situation by slogans such as "Franco and Perón are the world's best friends" and "What Marshall won't give us, Perón will."

There is little doubt that the economic help which Perón gave to Franco was one of the principal factors in making it possible for the Generalissimo to defy the United Nations. And it is noticeable that, when relations between Franco and Perón cooled in 1949 and Argentina refused to ship more goods to Spain without receiving payment in return, the Spanish regime was faced almost immediately with an economic crisis.

By the middle of 1950, Argentine-Spanish trade had come to a virtual standstill. The Argentines blamed the situation on the fact that Spain had failed to carry out its agreement to provide machinery and metal manufactures in return for Argentine wheat and cattle. Perhaps more fundamental was the fact that with the growing tightness of Argentina's exchange position, she no longer cared to finance Spanish purchases of cattle and grain. As a result Spain was purchasing these products elsewhere, Argentina was buying nothing from Spain, and relations between "El Caudillo" of Spain and "El Líder" of Argentina were very frigid. In any case, Perón no longer needed Franco's friendship.

The defiant attitude of the Perón regime towards the United Nations on the Spanish issue was no particular obstacle to the improvement of the Argentine position within the United Nations. To the great surprise of most observers, Argentina was elected as a member of the Security Council in the 1947 Assembly meeting. This was brought about by lobbying by Argentina among the Latin American countries in the United Nations. Having lined up sufficient support among them, Argentina was virtually assured of a position on the Council, since it was the tacit agreement in the United Nations that the Latin Americans should name their own regional members of the Security Council.

The Argentine representative on the Security Council, Foreign Minister Juan Bramuglia, made the most of his stay there. During his tenure of office as President of the Security Council—which, through the established system of rotation, came to Argentina in November, 1948—Bramuglia in a spectacular gesture tried to get the Russians and the Western Powers together on an agreement to end the Berlin blockade. Although he was not successful, he centered world attention on Argentina and on Argentina's would-be role as the world's peacemaker.

However, unfortunately for Argentine official policy, Foreign Minister Bramuglia was at this time in ill repute in his own country because of internal political difficulties. As a result, his name was not even mentioned in the Peronista press of Buenos Aires during the time when he was trying to resolve what was then the world's toughest problem, and the Argentine government did little to capitalize on the worldwide publicity which Bramuglia received. He resigned as foreign minister a few months later.

Although Bramuglia proved to be a prophet without honor in his own country, his actions did serve to emphasize the position which Perón had tried to carve for himself in world politics. Inside and outside of the United Nations, Perón attempted to establish himself as the leader of a "Third Bloc" in world affairs, which would have the task of mediating between Communist Russia on the one hand and Capitalist United States on the other. Perón took this line of argument and propaganda both at home and abroad. He told his fellow Argentines that he was the victim of attacks from both capitalists and Communists and therefore was the real spokesman for the "middle way"; while telling the world at large that he would like to unite all those who had no direct interest in the quarrel into a group which might mediate the dispute and avoid a Third World War.

The most dramatic effort in this direction was made by Perón in July, 1947, when he sent a message to all the countries of the earth. His message said in part:

The spiritual and material forces of Argentina are mobilized today to set forth to the world the decision of our country to aid humanity in the fulfillment of its aspiration for internal and international peace.

Our will and our spirit, inspired by the history of Argentina and America, wish to realize this aspiration.

Argentina wishes to place herself, through the awakening of her civic conscience, in a position from which she can help to achieve this universal claim. She aspires to contribute her effort to surmount the artificial obstacles created by man; to put an end to the anxiety of the destitute, and to ensure that the spirit and action of our country may always be at the service of the forces of good, to overcome the forces dominated by evil. . . .

The Argentine policy has been, is and always will be pacifist and generous.

The more concrete parts of the manifesto urged:

1. We call upon the peoples and governments of the world to

work for internal and international pacification as the only means to achieve the welfare of mankind.

2. Peoples and governments will achieve internal balance and peace respecting the rights inherent in the human personality, creating an economy of plenty, upholding the rights of the workers and organizing ways and means to further spiritual understanding.

3. People and governments must promote the factors leading to world balance, which they must base on mutual respect, juridical equality, obligatory arbitration, economic co-operation and permanent peace, to ensure international political normality, the economic security of the world, social justice on this earth and the pacification of spirits.

He followed this with a message to each of the presidents of American republics, urging them to join him in his efforts to mediate the world conflict. This message said in part:

International peace is the central problem mentioned in our call; rather than by the noble effort of the concert of nations and the determination of their governments, international peace must be consolidated by the popular will and must be maintained by the firm decision of hundreds of millions of men, transformed into zealous guardians of the purity of the universal pacifist principles, shortly to be materialized by the new will of those who have the duty of handing down to future generations a world stabilized by work and peace.

He outlined three steps which he said the American nations might take:

1. Firm adherence to the pacifist principles set forth.

2. The American nations and the Holy See must jointly address the remaining countries of the world, asking for their adherence to these pacifist principles and offer them the economic co-operation indispensable to the materialization of these aspirations cherished by the peoples of the earth.

3. Undertake to proclaim and realize these aspirations, theoretically and in practice, not only among states but also in international assemblies, conventions and meetings.

These two appeals had little effect on the course of events, but they did serve to further Perón's campaign of convincing the world that he stood for the "third way," which could steer between the two great warring factions into which the globe was divided.

However, this was not the only face which Perón put before the world. In international conferences he several times attempted to seize the leadership of the so-called "backward" nations and become their spokesman. This was notably true in the meetings of the Havana conference which established the International Trade Organization, in discussions on the establishment of an Inter-American Bank, and in the negotiations for an International Wheat Agreement.

In the Havana trade conference, Argentina took the lead in the bloc of nations opposing the position of the United States that barriers to commerce should be eliminated. Argentina, backed by most of the Latin American nations and by economically backward countries in other parts of the world, argued that the newly industrializing countries had to set up trade barriers in order to protect their growing industries. The Argentine delegates accused the United States of trying to destroy the nascent industries of Latin America, so that it would have a dumping ground for its manufactured products and thus could "export its unemployment."

Although not all of the backward countries went along with Argentina in all of the charges made against the motives of the United States, most did agree that they were not willing to destroy the elaborate systems of protection for "infant" industries which they had worked out and set in operation in the preceding decade and a half. As a result the United States was forced to make considerable concessions to their way of thinking, and, for practical purposes, the right of these countries to protect new and ultimately economic industries was recognized in the Havana Charter.

In discussions concerning the establishment of an Inter-American Development Bank, Argentina also was spokesman for the undeveloped countries against the United States. The idea of an Inter-American Bank was an old one. It had first been suggested in the 1930's and had actually been put into the form of a resolution at an Inter-American Conference; but the resolution had never been ratified by the necessary number of countries.

However, at each successive Inter-American meeting, the Argentines brought up the subject and finally, at the Havana Trade Conference early in 1948, Argentine Delegate Molinari offered five billion United States dollars for the economic development of Latin America. This proposal was elaborated upon by Miguel Miranda during a visit to Caracas, Venezuela, where he urged in a press conference the immediate creation of an Inter-American Bank and offered to have Argentina finance most of it. This proposal never became more than a boast, however, since the dollar squeeze was already beginning to be felt by Argentina.

Another international grandstand play, similar to the position on the Inter-American Bank, was the announcement by Argentine Ambassador to the United States Oscar Ivanissevich, in October, 1947, that Argentina had set up a "little Marshall Plan" to aid its Latin American neighbors. These neighbors, needless to say, heard little more of the matter.

In the negotiations over the International Wheat Agreement, the Argentines again spoke up as a representative of that group of nations which must export agricultural products and import most of their manufactured goods. Although Argentina did not have the international backing in these negotiations which she had in the Havana Conference, since she was the only really important Latin American participant, she took a line which pleased Latin American observers. In essence, Argentina saw no reason why she should agree to a restriction on the price of wheat, one of her main exports, when the industrial countries were making no moves to set top prices on the manufactured goods which Argentina and other predominantly agricultural countries must import.

Argentina put these ideas into practice in her dealings with Great Britain and other countries over the sale of her wheat, meat, corn, linseed, and other products. Her economic relations with Great Britain had been regulated from the beginning of the Second World War by a series of economic agreements or contracts between the governments of the two countries. The first of these was signed on October 23, 1939, and was intended to run for only sixteen weeks. However, other such agreements were made throughout the war; the fifth was signed by Britain in the name of all the United Nations. Argentina agreed in this contract to send the United Nations all its exportable surplus of refrigerated meats, which was defined as all meat left after taking the amount necessary for internal consumption and for shipment to other South American nations, and also Spain and Portugal. This pattern was followed in subsequent wartime contracts.

The first postwar agreement, signed on September 17, 1946, covered not only the question of meat but that of the balance of payments, the problem of the railroads, and the negotiation of a commercial treaty. In so far as meat was concerned, the British agreed to take all of Argentina's exportable surplus for four years, reserving to the Argentine government for sale in other markets 17 percent in the first year and 22 percent in the second and succeeding years. Prices were set at 45 percent above those in the first contract negotiated by the two countries. This agreement was supposed to run for four years, but it was invalidated by the decision of the British in the middle of 1947 to end convertibility of sterling.

The next agreement was the so-called Andes Convention, signed in February, 1948. This provided for the purchase not only of Argentine meat, but of other products such as corn, wheat, and linseed oil. The United Kingdom for its part agreed to supply Argentina with certain manufactured goods and fuel. The remainder of Britain's commercial debt to Argentina was to be covered by the transfer of British-owned railroads in Argentina to the Argentine government.

This contract did not call for Britain to take all of Argentina's excess production of meat. Instead, a certain money value of meat was to be bought, at prices arranged in the accord. A clearing account was maintained in the Bank of England and the Argentine Central Bank; the surplus was expendable anywhere in the sterling area.

The latest in this series of accords was signed in 1949 to run until 1954. Both governments agreed to use all possible means to increase trade between the two countries, with the objective of maintaining an equal balance at as high a level as possible. Prices for meat were set at 97 pounds ten shillings per long ton (as opposed to 76 pounds in the previous agreement), and a provision was made that prices were to be reexamined each year following a four-month period of negotiations.

The Argentines were highly pleased with this accord, since, they maintained, it would allow them, for the first time, to purchase all their coal and petroleum needs without recourse to dollars. In addition, the United Kingdom agreed to provide iron, steel, and products manufactured from them; other metals and metal products; chemicals, drugs, and the like machinery; textiles, hardware; ceramics, and other manufactured products.

Although this and previous agreements gratified the Argentines, they did not please their British customers. The London *Economist* indicated discontent with Argentine prices when, in its February, 1949, issue it urged the government to cut the meat ration rather than agree to the terms which Argentina was then offering. It said: "Such a reduction would impose a hardship on the British public, but it would be worth while if it deflated, once for all, Argentina's bargaining power."

Early in 1950 the young British Minister of Foods, Maurice Webb, referred to the treatment which Britain had received from Argentina as "blackmail." The Argentine government pretended to be shocked at this statement—but did not break off negotiations for the 1950–1951 prices.

Other countries protested against the high prices which Argentina charged for her products in the period after the Second World War. Said the sedate *El Mercurio* of Santiago, Chile, in commenting on the 43 percent increase in cattle prices, which the Argentine government decreed in 1948: "We must resign ourselves either to pay these prices or to get along with less meat." In the case of Brazil, the Argentines raised the price of wheat from 14.5 pesos a quintal in March, 1946, to 15.5 in April of that year and then increased it to 30 pesos by the end of 1946. At the close of 1947, Argentine wheat was costing Brazilians 60 pesos a quintal. These price boosts were bitterly resented in Rio de Janeiro and were interpreted by many as a move to influence Brazilians against President Dutra.

However, by the end of 1949 the shoe was on the other foot; British negotiators threatened to denounce the 1949 treaty if the Argentine prices were not more reasonable. Negotiations on prices for the 1950–1951 period were stalemated beyond the July 1, 1950, deadline date. By the end of April, 1951, an agreement had still not been reached.

The chief factor in weakening the Argentine bargaining position was the fact that Argentina was confronted by a very serious lack of foreign exchange. The country's gold and dollar reserves fell from 1,700,000,000 pesos in January, 1947, to only 600,000,000 in August, 1948. In addition, the country owed some 1,200,000,000 pesos to American banks. In a move to escape this dilemma, the government lowered the value of the peso from four to the dollar to 4.85 in June, 1948. This scheme brought only temporary relief.

By 1950, Argentina was very short of sterling as well as of dollars. The Banco Central announced in April, 1950, that its holdings of sterling had dropped from 60 million pounds in June, 1949, to only 12 million, ten months later, a decline which even British observers agreed was dangerously swift.

The reasons for this shortage of foreign currency are not hard to find. Available dollars had been spent on importing goods needed for the Armed Forces, the Five Year Plan, and for consumption. Sterling credits, accumulated as a result of huge sales to Britain of wheat, cattle, linseed, and other products, were for the most part canceled by purchases of goods from Britain under the annual trade agreements, by repatriation of Argentina's foreign debt, and by purchase of British owned public utilities and railroads.

Sales of Argentine goods in many other countries were subsidized by the Argentine government itself. Large credits were extended to a number of nations, including France, Spain, Portugal, Finland, and Czechoslovakia, for the purchase of Argentine agricultural products. In at least some of these cases there was little chance of immediate repayment; therefore the sales did not mean that Argentina received other goods in return or foreign currencies with which she could purchase needed products in third countries.

The result of all of this was that receipts by Argentina in 1948 amounted to only 5.8 billion pesos (mainly gained from exports), whereas expenditures for imports, debt service, and other items were 5.6 billion pesos. This surplus on current account of 200,000 pesos compared unfavorably with a surplus of 600 million in 1947 and 1.4 billion in 1946. Moreover, a category of "special expenditures" (accounted for mainly by the purchase of the British railways), amounted to some two billion pesos, leaving the net deficit for the year at 1.8 billion pesos, as contrasted with a net deficit of one billion pesos in 1947 and a surplus of 200 million in 1946.

After the devaluation of the British pound, the Argentine government introduced an involved system of variable exchange rates. These official rates varied from 9.40 pesos, used for British purchases of Argentine meat under the 1949 agreement, to 25.27, the rate at which the Banco Central would sell sterling to people in Argentina wishing to make a remittance to the United Kingdom. At the same time, absolute restrictions on imports were established; under these only given amounts of certain items could be imported from particular countries. These restrictions were so set up that Argentine importers were forced to buy from countries which were buying from Argentina.

As a result of the refusal of the Perón government to issue import licenses and make exchange available for many types of imports, the Argentines were very slow in fulfilling the provisions of the 1949 Anglo-Argentine accord calling for Argentine purchase of British goods.

Importers of goods classified by the government as "unessential" were only allowed to obtain foreign exchange at infrequent intervals through a system of "auctioning" of foreign currencies. This "auctioning" was designed to net the government the largest possible return and at the same time to act as a damper on the importation of "unessential" products. Early in 1950 two auctions of foreign currency were held by the Argentine government. The result of the first was kept secret, but it is known that, in the second, some two million pounds sterling were offered. The auction price for this sterling, according to the London *Economist,* was 33.47 pesos to the pound for goods listed as unessential imports in Category A, and 37.22 pesos to the pound for those in Category B.

Devaluation of the peso gave Argentina some temporary relief in the latter months of 1949. The Ministry of Economy announced in November that most of the stocks of goods in I.A.P.I. warehouses had been sold. United States importers took the largest amount, while Western European nations purchased most of the rest. The Ministry of Economy claimed that the adjustments accompanying the devaluation had brought Argentine export prices into line with international prices.

However, the continued seriousness of the Argentine shortage of foreign exchange is shown by the comment of the *Economist* on March 4, 1950:

Every few days since the beginning of the year, trade negotiators from various overseas countries have been arriving in Buenos Aires with long lists of goods they are willing to sell and buy— only to run against the difficulty that Argentina, with its meat and wheat bespoken and its maize crop ruined by drought, has little except vegetable oils to offer in exchange.

Argentina sought relief from this situation through bilateral barter agreements. One such accord, signed with Portugal in October, 1949, provided for the exchange of products valued at about two million United States dollars, and pledged the two countries to maintain a balanced trade. A similar agreement with Australia in April, 1950, called for the exchange of a total of about £1,000,000 worth of goods.

As a result of the economic crisis, symbolized by inflation and shortage of foreign exchange, Perón was unable to follow through on the grandiose ideas which he had proposed and propagandized during the first two or three years of his administration: the Inter-American Development Bank, and the series of treaties of economic union and commercial relations suggested to his neighbors in 1946–1947.

Economic treaties were proposed to Chile, Paraguay, and Bolivia. These were very broad agreements, providing for the abolition of customs barriers between Argentina and the specified country, the investment of considerable sums of money by Argentina, and the development in the nations particularly involved of mineral and other resources, which Argentina's new industrial program would need. The upshot of the adoption and implementation of these agreements would have been the formation of an economic bloc of the southern South American countries, dominated by Argentina as the industrial center of a group of raw-material-producing satellites.

There was long and bitter discussion over these proposed agreements in the countries involved. Certain aspects of the accord with Bolivia were adopted by the Bolivian Congress. In Chile, there was a long discussion in the Congress before a final refusal to ratify the accord. Internal politics were partly responsible for the rejection of a treaty with Chile, but the discussions also revealed much resentment against, and distrust of, Perón's Argentina. Many Chileans feared that their country would become nothing more than a producer of raw materials for Argentina and that Chile's own industrialization program would be brought to a halt. The Chileans also feared too close political entanglement with Argentina, a nation stronger and more populous than theirs.

The Chileans had good reason for fearing the Perón regime. On several occasions the Peronista regime has used economic force in an attempt to bring its neighbors to heel. For instance, in the case of Uruguay, Perón was upset by the fact that that country was the principal refuge for Argentine political exiles, who, from across the Rio de la Plata, carried on constant attacks and organizational efforts against the Perón regime. In April, 1946, in an effort to punish the Uruguayan regime for harboring Perón's political enemies, the Argentine government refused to ship any more wheat to Uruguay. This threat was met by the offer by the United States to ship Uruguay the needed grain.

General Perón again used wheat as a weapon to weaken the efforts of President Dutra to reestablish a democratic regime in Brazil. Perón pushed the price of the grain to such heights that a large increase in the price of bread in Brazil became inevitable, thus increasing unrest among Brazilian workers. Brazilians were also disturbed by the fact that late in 1946 Perón ordered that the regular spring Army maneuvers be held within a few miles of the Brazilian border. As a result, the Brazilian army was reported to have rushed considerable reinforcements to the region.

In the case of another neighbor, Bolivia, in July, 1946, Perón instituted a blockade of the mutual frontier in reprisal against the overthrow of the Bolivian government of Major Villarroel, with which he had been on friendly terms.

All these events strengthened the suspicions of some of Perón's South American neighbors that Argentina under his direction was becoming "imperialistic." They could not help but remember that he had been the reported head of the sinister G.O.U., which, a few weeks before the coup of June, 1943, had frankly proclaimed its desire to establish Argentine hegemony over South America.

Perón has felt called upon several times to deny any imperialistic ambitions. In a speech delivered before a group of visiting Brazilian students, he said:

It has been said that we wish to reconstruct the Viceroyalty of the Rio de la Plata [the Spanish colonial administrative division which included Argentina, Uruguay, Southern Brazil, Paraguay and part of Bolivia—R.A.]. When this is said I think of those regions which would form it, and I answer: "We have a great deal of land; we need no more." Then I think of the economies of those areas which would belong to it. Everyone knows that these are for the most part deficit regions. It would be bad business, then, to rebuild the Viceroyalty of the Rio de la Plata.

Are we imperialists, with 16,000,000 inhabitants? Our imperialism consists in constructing with Argentine labor and sacrifice a better country than we found, to hand it on to those who come after us.

In spite of this disclaimer by Perón, some of his subordinates have quite frankly advocated the reestablishment of the old Viceroyalty. In a book written in 1946, Lucio M. Moreno Quintana, Subsecretary of Foreign Relations under the *de facto* government, proclaimed this one of the three principal objects of Peronista foreign policy. In a speech before the National College of Buenos Aires in April, 1947, Moreno Quintana once again argued that "The Argentine Republic must come to include not only the territory within its present boundaries but also the Republics of Uruguay, Paraguay, Bolivia and the southern part of Brazil." This speech was published in the official bulletin of the Peronista-controlled University of Buenos Aires.

Oppositionists, too, are convinced of the aggressive intentions of the Peronista regime. Ousted Radical Deputy Colonel Attilio Cataneo has stated:

Argentina under the government of General Perón not only has expressed geo-political sentiments, but its armament plans are an unequivocal complement of the totalitarian ambitions of the government. Its agreements with neighboring governments are frankly imperialistic and fit into the geo-political and totalitarian plans of the regime.

Whatever his imperial ambitions may be, it is certain that Perón is a vigorous Argentine nationalist. As such, he has accomplished a great deal during his first five years in office to raise the prestige and position of his country in world affairs. Whether or not he will go on from there to attempt to subjugate his neighbors only time can tell.

PERONISMO FOR EXPORT

THE DUCE used to calm worried believers in the self-determination of nations by false assurances that "fascism is not for export." So far as this author knows, the Argentine "Líder" has made no such assertions about Peronismo. In fact, there is plenty of evidence that he regards his political movement as something which *is* for export and that he is doing his best to spread it abroad.

Peronismo has been exported on three distinct levels: labor, general publicity, and military. Through his kept labor movement and the labor services of his government, Perón has attempted to sell the Peronista brand of labor relations to workers of other American countries. Moreover, he has not hesitated to try to impress his point of view on the general public of Latin America. And, finally, through military connections, his regime has tried to peddle a somewhat different brand of product.

Soon after the "descamisados" voted him into the presidency, Perón conceived the idea of setting himself up as a Hemispheric protector of the workingman. His first step was to place labor attachés in every Argentine legation and embassy in the New World. Second-rank Peronista labor leaders were trained for these jobs in a special school in Buenos Aires, where the keystone of the curriculum was a basic survey course in Peronismo. Lectures on "The Personality of Perón," and "Principles of Peronismo" took up most of the students' remaining time.

When President Perón started his crusade to win friends and influence people in other American labor movements, his standing in the rest of the hemisphere was very bad. At several meetings of the International Labor Organization in 1945 and 1946 there were moves to unseat the Argentine workers' delegates on the grounds that they did not really speak for their fellow workers, but rather were representatives of the government.

Perón's labor attachés have made considerable progress in wooing other union groups. The first Argentine labor attaché in Chile promptly visited both factions of the then violently feuding Confederation of Workers of Chile and showed no favoritism. The nice things he had to say about both were published in the press of each faction, since both welcomed whatever support they could muster. That the Argentine labor attachés in Chile succeeded in ingratiating themselves with Chilean labor leaders is demonstrated by the fact that a dinner given by Attaché Alejandro Jatar for Chilean trade union leaders early in 1950 was very well attended.

The effect of the activities of the Argentine labor attaché in Colombia is reflected in excerpts from a letter received by the author in 1948 from a leading anti-Peronista labor leader of Colombia, who said:

. . . Señor Pedro Otero, the labor attaché of the Argentine Embassy, as well as other functionaries of the Embassy and even the Ambassador himself, has been visiting the unions, federations, and even the C.T.C. and has also been seeing the union leaders individually. He offers them scholarships, and invites them to visit Argentina, as well as giving them pamphlets. These Argentine diplomats have been making numerous social calls on labor leaders; they have a regular radio program each week, they have been participating in the organization of the Colombian Social Security System, and they have been extending their influence among Colombian youth by offering scholarships in Argentine industrial schools, specialized institutes and the like. . . . The workers are going with increasing frequency to the Argentine embassy where they not only receive numerous magazines, pamphlets, and other reading material, but are treated with the utmost courtesy and attention. . . . The Argentines have invited all the leaders of the Confederation of Workers of Colombia, the Federation of White Collar Workers, and various newspaper men to go to Argentina. At the present moment brother ——, a well-known anti-Communist trade unionist, is just leaving for Argentina. I do not think that he will return here as good a friend of ours as he has been.

In Peru the attaché failed to gain acceptance from the Confederation of Workers of Peru, controlled by the Aprista Party, but he did become very friendly with one small opposition group, the so-called Independent Trade Union Committee, headed by a conglomeration of ex-Communists and ex-Apristas. When the Confederation of Workers and the Apristas were outlawed in October, 1948, after a military coup, the Argentine-advised labor group was favored by the new military dictatorship. The Argentine attaché is reputed to have had much to do with framing new "social legislation" for the regime.

The Argentine underground Socialist newspaper *La Vanguardia* published in August, 1949, a protest by the leaders of the Confederation of Workers of Peru against the activities of the Argentine labor attaché in Peru:

The Conference of Peruvian Workers denounces to the workers of this country and abroad the interventionist activities of the Argentine Embassy in Lima in internal Peruvian affairs, not only in the realm of politics but in the trade union field as well. Through enticement, persuasion and bribery, trade union functionaries are being lured to the Argentine Embassy where they are offered trips to Buenos Aires with all expenses paid by the Argentine government. In other cases, they are sending these trade union leaders to the Trade Union School established by the Perón regime to serve its ends in both internal and foreign policy. . . . The same Argentine embassy urges the workers whom it snares to give their utmost support to the totalitarian government which is now ruling Peru, whose affinity to the regime of Perón is not hidden.

The attachés not only try to curry favor with union leaders, but often go directly to the rank and file. In Ecuador, for instance, the Peronista representative has lectured frequently before Catholic labor organizations. In Costa Rica, the author attended a meeting of a local branch of the Confederation of Labor held in honor of Padre Benjamin Nuñez, who had resigned as secretary of the Confederation to become minister of labor. The Argentine labor attaché, who already knew some of the local union leaders, turned up uninvited. Out of courtesy he was asked to sit on the platform and finally was called upon for a few words. He told of the latest wonders that had been performed in Argentina, and pointedly announced that Evita Perón had just sent a large consignment of clothing for the poor of Costa Rica.

In Costa Rica, incidentally, the Peronistas won the support of the president of the Confederation of Labor who was subsequently ousted from his post, but only after a serious fight within the organization. In July, 1950, the Peronista element actually forced the resignation of the democratic members of the Executive of the Confederation. However, in a convention of the Confederation held two weeks later the Peronistas were completely defeated, and a resolution was passed empowering the new Executive Committee elected by the Convention to oust all Peronistas from the organization. The Peronistas subsequently formed another federation.

Argentine labor attachés have often been accused of engaging in activities quite different from the avowed aim of spreading good will. Union leaders in certain countries are reported to have received money from Argentine sources. On this point there is little direct evidence, but a few facts are known. In Havana, the labor paper *Acción Socialista* began carrying advertisements for the Argentine airline soon after the arrival of Perón's attaché—though FAMA did not at that time run to Havana. The attaché in Mexico offered to pay the way of a Mexican delegation to the January, 1948, congress in Lima, Peru, which founded the C.I.T. (Inter-American Confederation of Workers). This was done in the hope that the Mexicans would take the part of the Peronista unions at the meeting. The cost of a further trip to Buenos Aires was also offered; both proposals are said to have been rejected, though the trade union leader in question did support the Peronistas in Lima and did go on to Buenos Aires.

In yet another case, in Haiti, a trade union leader publishes a weekly paper which is loaded with fulsome praise of Perón, Evita, the C.G.T., and everything Argentine. The publisher of this paper also founded and headed the Argentine-Haitian Friendship Society. The paper has only a small, scattered circulation and certainly could not be published without support from somewhere. A process of elimination—together with the paper's editorial policy—leads to the Argentine embassy. The publisher of this paper was one of the labor leaders making a trip to Buenos Aires, with all expenses paid by the Argentine government.

Perón has arranged elaborate pilgrimages to Buenos Aires for quite a few leaders of Latin American trade unions. The first such excursion was made by some of the delegates to the C.I.T.'s Lima conference. This trip was so successful that in May, 1948, a larger delegation of union chiefs was brought to Argentina. Thereafter, smaller groups of workers—and sometimes individuals—from other Latin American countries were brought to view the glories of Perón's Argentina. For example, a delegation of railroad workers from Ecuador was wined and dined for a week early in 1950, and a group of paper workers from Chile was brought over in May, 1950, to attend the convention of the Argentine Paper Workers Union.

Not all of these visiting workers were convinced. Two Socialists from Ecuador somewhat rudely made speeches attacking the Peron regime while they were still in Buenos Aires. They made the obvious but sometimes overlooked point that the Peronistas were destroying all labor organizations that would not take orders. A Costa Rican trade union leader made a similar charge upon his return home.

The Peronistas caused considerable commotion at the January, 1951, meeting in Mexico City which organized the American affiliate of the International Confederation of Free Trade Unions. Certain Mexican unions were in favor of admitting the Argentine C.G.T. to the new American Regional Organization of Workers, and they invited the C.G.T. to send a delegation. After a bitter debate the delegates refused to seat the Argentine Peronista delegates, and the representatives of the Confederation of Workers of Mexico (C.T.M.) walked out in protest.

After this refusal to admit the C.G.T. to the I.C.F.T.U. conference, the Peronista delegates were the chief speakers at a protest meeting, where the platform was shared by representatives of the Mexican C.R.O.M. confederation. There was much talk about forming a hemispheric Peronista confederation of labor. However, neither at this meeting nor in the months thereafter was anything concrete done to carry this threat (or promise?) into execution.

Whether or not they succeed in forming a hemispheric federation, it is certain that pro-Perón groups have sprung up in many of the national labor movements. In Peru the labor-group favored by the dictatorship of President Odría works closely with Perón. Early in 1949, President Odría gave the Peruvian delegate to a white-collar workers' conference in Buenos Aires a warm personal sendoff. In Ecuador, Perón's influence is strongest in the Catholic labor movement. In Panama, the largest of three labor confederations is favorably inclined toward the Argentine dictatorship. In Mexico, Uruguay, Costa Rica, and Haiti there are active and, in some cases, important labor groups friendly to the Peronistas.

However, Perón has not been content to work only among the trade unionists, but has sought wider influence on public opinion. Jaunts similar to those arranged for Latin American labor leaders were also offered to students, teachers, and others who might be able to gain adherents for Perón. The paper *Diario da Noite* in Rio de Janeiro, Brazil, commented on these visits, saying, "Thus Perón hopes to form groups of admirers of both him personally and of Argentina, who later can be transformed into full-blown agents of Peronismo in their respective countries." It is reported that, up to the early part of 1950, more than 5,000 Brazilians had been brought to Argentina on all-expense tours.

The Argentine regime has even attempted to influence radio broadcasters in several countries. The opposition paper *Argentina Libre* reported on January 21, 1949, that three Uruguayan radio stations noted for their pro-Perón line in reporting events were subsidized by the Peronistas. The Uruguayan daily *El Pais* reported on November 7, 1948, that Argentines "closely associated with the government" had purchased two radio stations in the interior of the country.

In Cuba, Senator Eduardo Chíbas said of the Peronista activities there: "In Cuba, Peronismo is hard at work, underground of course, since one does not conspire in the light of day." He accused the Argentines of attempting to control the important Cuban radio network Cadena Azul through the payment of a sum of $250,000 a year for four years, so as to use this radio station as a center of Peronista propaganda in the Caribbean area.

In Brazil, the Argentines tried unsuccessfully to get the principal radio broadcasters to use the facilities of the Argentine government's Agencia Noticiosa Argentina news agency.

The press in neighboring countries has not been entirely neglected. In Chile, soon after Perón's inauguration there began to appear *El Laborista,* a paper enthusiastically supporting Perón and urging the need of a similar kind of regime in Chile. This paper did not have any lasting success. However, there are undoubtedly other publicity organs in various Latin American countries which have been subject to the blandishments of the Perón regime.

The Peronistas have even tried to gain support among Catholic clergymen in neighboring countries. The Chilean magazine *Ercilla* reported in April, 1949, that numerous Chilean priests had been deluged with Peronista propaganda. At least one important Chilean cleric, the Coadjutant Vicar of Andacollo, refused to open the package of Peronista literature he received, saying "I consider it unfortunate that we are sent political propaganda."

Even international conferences have not been overlooked by the crusading Peronistas as a means of gaining general Latin American support for their regime. For instance, at a continental congress on Indian Affairs in Cuzco, Peru, in 1949, the Argentine Ambassador to Peru, who headed the Argentine delegation to the conference, introduced a motion expressing admiration and support for the "peace efforts" of Sra. Perón. Although he finally withdrew the motion, a great deal of time and parliamentary maneuver was wasted on the issue. A bit later he prepared another motion to the effect that all codes of social legislation in the Americas should be modified to conform to the principles set forth in the new Peronista constitution. When this met with a cold reception, the Argentine delegates, undismayed, introduced another suggestion: that such legislation should include a number of specifications—all of which are listed in the Peronista Constitution. This suggestion was finally accepted, with a modification appending a proviso that "freedom of organization by the workers" should also be assured by all American social labor legislation. This modification was accepted over the objections of the Argentine delegate.

A good deal more serious than this kind of exportation of Peronismo are the contacts of the Peronistas with military men throughout the continent. Numerous military uprisings and would-be uprisings since 1943 have been attributed to the undercover influence of the Peronista forces in Argentina. It is said that the G.O.U. of Argentina was very active in aiding the establishment of similar secret lodges in the armies of other countries. A writer in the opposition paper *Realidad Argentina*, in January, 1949, attributed to the proselytizing activities of the Argentine Grupo de Oficiales Unidos the formation of the Grupo de Oficiales Seleccionados (G.O.S.) in Chile, the Logia Mariscal Santa Cruz in Bolivia, and the Logia Frente de Guerra in Paraguay.

In Chile in December, 1948, the First Secretary of the Argentine Embassy, L. Zervino, and Consul General Tixi Massa were declared *persona non grata* by the Chilean government for allegedly participating in a plot with various Chilean military figures. In 1949, Chilean Socialist Senator Salvador Allende accused the Argentine government of inspiring "military coups—which are surrounding Chile with an iron curtain of military dictatorships."

In Cuba, Senator Eddy Chíbas reported late in 1948 that Perón's roving missionary, Senator Molinari, had been distributing watches and other gifts to garrison commanders in some of the Cuban provinces.

The activities of the Peronista military men gained most

attention at the time of the overthrow of the governments of
Peru and Venezuela by military coups in October and November, 1948. It was known that General Odría, who headed
the Peruvian revolt, had often been in Argentina and was an
admirer of Perón. Drew Pearson reported that Odría had consulted at length with the Argentine Ambassador in Lima before carrying out his coup.

Colonel Pérez Jiménez, one of the two principal figures in
the Venezuelan coup, was not only a former student of Odría
at the Peruvian Military College, but also had been in Argentina only two or three months before helping to overthrow
the Venezuelan government of President Gallegos. During
this visit, Pérez Jiménez had received a high decoration from
Perón.

Ex-President Rómulo Betancourt of Venezuela filed official
charges with the United Nations in February, 1949, alleging
that the Argentine military attaché in Caracas had played a
prominent part in the upset of the democratically elected
government. He said, "There is in America a 'Reactionary International' headed by Argentina and General Perón." The
Argentine Ambassador to Venezuela denied these charges, of
course.

In the case of the Bolivian revolution of December, 1943,
the connection is a bit more obvious. A Father Wilkinson,
who was closely associated with the Argentine *de facto* government, was reported to have traveled constantly between
Argentina and La Paz, Bolivia, taking money and advice to
the Bolivian revolutionaries. Perón is said to have relayed the
news of Villarroel's victory in Bolivia to then War Minister
Farrell of Argentina with the words, "We have just triumphed
in Bolivia."

The Argentines have been accused of intervention in subsequent upheavals in Bolivia. It is known that for some
months after the overthrow of Villarroel in July, 1946, Perón

instituted a boycott of Bolivia and refused to allow Argentines to export food and other materials there. And in the middle of 1949 when Bolivia was in the throes of civil war, the rebels came from across the Argentine border and went back across it when they were defeated. The Bolivian government sent an official protest to Argentina for aiding the rebels.

Two other neighboring countries have also been subject to interference by Perón. He has maintained close relations with various military groups in Paraguay, and during that country's civil war in 1947 took a friendly attitude toward the government of President Morinigo—one of the main reasons for its triumph. In Uruguay, Argentine Peronistas have worked closely with the opposition Nationalist or Herrerista party. Emissaries have gone back and forth between the two groups and Herreristas have been ostentatiously received by Perón.

Five years after his inauguration, Perón was still actively seeking followers in other Latin American countries. In the first years of his administration, his efforts to become "El Líder" of the continent were enhanced by the virtually unlimited amounts of money available. Even after the foreign exchange situation began to tighten, Perón continued to spend sizable amounts on "missionary work" abroad.

JUAN DOMINGO AND TIO SAM

SINCE JUNE 4, 1943, the relations between Argentina and the United States have been marked by an inconsistency of conduct on the part of the United States that has bewildered casual observers, gravely disillusioned Argentine democrats, and made skeptical the other peoples and governments of the hemisphere. American conduct has varied from violent antagonism to slavish ingratiation. On the other hand, the conduct of the *de facto* and Perón governments has been consistent, though occasionally marked by some diplomatic retreats. The consistent stand of the Argentine government thus far has been antagonism toward Tío Sam (as the Latin Americans call their powerful northern "uncle"), coupled with a determination to get as much out of him as possible.

Prior to June 4, 1943, the United States had been uneasy about the policies of the Castillo government. President Castillo made little secret of his admiration for Mussolini and especially for Franco, and did little to align his nation with the United Nations or even to take any moves against Nazi plotting within Argentina's own boundaries.

In the Emergency Conference of American States which met in Rio de Janeiro in January, 1942, to decide on common policies in view of the attack on Pearl Harbor and the subsequent involvement of a number of the American nations in the Second World War, Argentina took the lead in opposing every proposal put forward by the United States. This country was at that time eager to have the Latin Americans break off diplomatic relations with the Axis and take moves against spying and other anti-Allied activities. Argentina—followed for a while by Chile—virtually refused to do this, and it was not until early in 1944 that she finally broke off diplomatic ties with the Axis powers. Even then comparatively little was done against Axis espionage and propaganda activities.

In view of this negative attitude on the part of the Castillo regime, the United States government was very happy to see the overthrow of the obstinate Argentine chief executive. With the wisdom of hindsight it seems now that the United States authorities were prematurely jubilant, paying entirely too little attention to who it was that had overthrown the Castillo government. With almost unseemly haste, the United States recognized the new provisional regime of General Ramírez. At the time, Ramírez and others gave out sometimes conflicting, but never very definite, statements concerning their attitude toward the Axis. There were reports that they were preparing not only to break off diplomatic relations but to join in on the Allied side. There were other reports to the contrary, and many experienced Argentine politicians were very skeptical about the supposed United Nations sympathies of the new rulers of their country. Nevertheless, the United States had quickly extended recognition.

Once recognition was gained, the military regime in Argentina took its own time about showing any particular enthusiasm for the Allies. American ardor for the new regime began to cool. With the occurrence of another military revolution in Argentina's neighbor, Bolivia, on December 21, 1943, in which avowedly pro-Nazi elements were involved, the United States became increasingly wary. It implied that the Argentine regime had had its hand in the Bolivian affair, and instituted consultations among the other American republics to determine a common course of action concerning the recognition of the new Bolivian government. It was indeed some months before the United States and most other American governments gave the government of Major Villarroel its official nod. Argentina had no such compunctions, recognizing the new regime on January 4, 1944.

The overthrow of General Ramírez and his substitution by General Farrell in February, 1944, gave the United States a chance for another switch in diplomatic attitude toward the *de facto* government. The overthrow of Ramírez came only a few days after his government had severed relations with the Axis and made pronouncements indicating that the country was going to line up on the side of the United Nations. (By that time, the outcome of the war was becoming clear.) For this reason, if for no other, the United States government felt that there was something a little peculiar about the overthrow of Ramírez. In all probability, however, the war issue was only one reason for the ousting of General Ramírez—his succession by General Farrell meant that the Perón clique was seizing charge of the revolution and of the government.

After the overthrow of Ramírez, the United States began consultations with other American nations concerning recognition of the Farrell government. However, while these were still in progress, Acting Secretary of State Edward Stettinius announced that the American Ambassador had been instructed to avoid entering into official relations with the new government, "pending further developments." This state of diplomatic suspended animation continued for three months, during which the United States Ambassador was present in Buenos Aires but was not accredited to the Farrell government.

In June, 1944, the United States sent a memorandum to all the other American republics save Argentina, saying that the time had come for an end to the Argentine impasse and submitting a report on events since Farrell had come to power. This report indicated that the Farrell government was giving the Axis ex-diplomats free rein to travel at will and do what they wished in Argentina, that Axis spies had been released from jail, and that the Farrell government had requisitioned critical materials from pro-Allied firms and had given financial support to a number of pro-Axis papers.

The note ended with the announcement that the United States was withdrawing its ambassador to Buenos Aires and suggested that if all other American republics would withdraw their ambassadors within two weeks, it would make a great impression on the Argentine administration. All the American countries except Chile, Bolivia, and Paraguay complied soon afterward; the United Kingdom acted similarly. This slap at the Farrell regime was made more stinging by the fact that the day after the withdrawal of the United States Ambassador from Buenos Aires the United States and eighteen Latin American countries recognized the government of Major Villarroel in Bolivia.

With these actions commenced what was perhaps the most unfriendly period of Argentine-American relations in the history of the two nations. For over a year the United States refused to recognize the validity of General Farrell's seizure of power, and kept up a constant barrage against the Argentine government, implying or charging outright that it was seeking to aid the Axis powers. On September 30, 1944, President Roosevelt himself issued a statement condemning "Nazi-Fascist influence" in Argentina. Argentina was accused of giving refuge to fleeing Axis leaders.

Occasionally, the Argentine government struck back. For instance, late in 1944 the Argentine Minister of Foreign Affairs sent a note to the Pan American Union asking for a consultative meeting of the Foreign Ministers of the American

Republics to give Argentina a chance to disprove the charges of the United States against her. Seriously embarrassed by this move the United States tried to prevail upon the other Latin American republics to declare against such a meeting. However, their united pressure for the meeting forced United States acquiescence to it, and the Chapultepec Conference of the American republics was the result.

Before the Chapultepec Conference convened in February, 1945, secret meetings took place between United States representatives and Argentine leaders, including Farrell, Perón, Foreign Minister Cooke, and others. The upshot of these discussions was that, if Argentina would implement her hemispheric anti-Axis commitments agreed to in the Rio de Janeiro Conference of 1942, the United States would drop its coercive attitude toward the Farrell regime.

The chief accomplishments of the Chapultepec Conference were two: the Act of Chapultepec, declaring that an attack on any American state by an American or extra-American power was an attack on all the others; and a United States–Argentine accord. The essence of the accord was that Argentina would declare war on the Axis and tighten restrictions on Axis activities in Argentina; in return, the United States would use its influence to secure the admission of Argentina into the United Nations at the forthcoming San Francisco Conference.

At the San Francisco Conference the United States was seriously embarrassed by its advocacy of admission of Argentina. Some complicated political maneuvering took place among the assembled powers. At Yalta, President Roosevelt had agreed to the admission of the constituent Soviet republics of White Russia and the Ukraine as sovereign members of the United Nations. The Latin Americans consented to this arrangement on the condition that Argentine also be admitted. At a secret meeting in San Francisco attended by the

Big Four Foreign Ministers as well as those of Brazil, Chile, and Mexico, Molotov agreed to Argentina's being seated— on the condition that the Russian-sponsored but generally unrecognized Polish government of Lublin also be accepted.

Great Britain and the United States could not agree to the seating of the Lublin government, so Molotov then claimed that he was not sufficiently familiar with the Argentine situation to support the admission of Argentina. In the full sessions of the Conference Molotov violently, if unsuccessfully, opposed Argentine admission, accusing the United States of supporting fascism in the form of the Farrell government. Characteristically enough, at that very time, Russian delegates were meeting Argentine representatives in São Paulo, Brazil, for the purpose of establishing the bases for diplomatic recognition and a commercial treaty.

Subsequent to the San Francisco Conference, the United States decided to grant its long-delayed recognition of the Farrell government. As the man to reestablish relations, President Truman chose Spruille Braden. Braden was the son of one of the world's greatest copper magnates, but no longer had any financial interest in the Braden Copper Company. He had been a diplomat during the Second World War, serving as ambassador to Colombia and to Cuba; in Cuba, he had won considerable prestige by sternly ordering American businessmen to keep their hands off the Cuban presidential election of 1944.

Braden was not sent down to Argentina to "make up" with the Farrell regime, but rather to make it very clear to the Argentine people that the United States government did not like that regime for the reason that General Farrell, Colonel Perón and their associates had been friends and co-workers with the late-lamented Axis and were menaces to democracy in the hemisphere. Braden also was to indicate that he hoped that Farrell, Perón and Co. would soon meet the fate of their German and Italian models.

On his arrival in Argentina, Braden began an undiplomatic but frank campaign against the Farrell regime's suppression of civil liberties and its friendship with the Axis powers. He made speech after speech attacking the Argentine government, by direct reference, by implication, and by innuendo. He started this campaign in an interview with Vice President Perón soon after his arrival on July 7, when he demanded press freedom, and lodged specific complaints against the treatment accorded United States correspondents in Argentina. There could not be good relations between the two countries, warned Braden, while the press was suppressed, political prisoners remained in jail, and Axis activities in Argentina remained uncontrolled.

Braden maintained extremely friendly relations with anti-Peronista politicians. The doors of the American Embassy were wide open for the leaders and members of the Radical, Socialist, Progressive Democratic, and Conservative parties. And these political leaders made little secret of the fact that they approved of the activities of Mr. Braden and believed the validity of the charges which he was making against Farrell, Perón, and the others. There was no doubt—at the time— about the opposition politicians' approval of the activities of the American Ambassador.

However, Braden's stay in Argentina was not to be a long one. He was promoted to Assistant Secretary of State late in August, 1945, and left Argentina in September. The Peronistas immediately interpreted his removal as a defeat for his policies and as a victory for them. His departure was followed almost immediately by the reimposition of the state of siege, which had been lifted six weeks earlier as a partial response to the Braden campaign.

After his departure, and after the—for the opposition—disastrous election of February, 1946, opinion was very much divided, even among the anti-Peronistas, as to whether the Americans had been wise to have their Ambassador make quite such an open campaign against Perón and the Argentine government of the time. Some felt that Braden had intervened a little too openly in the internal affairs of Argentina, and that the natural resentment of Argentine citizens against this interference by the Colossus of the North had been sufficient to turn the electoral tide in favor of Perón.

On the other hand, there were those among the opposition who continued to feel that Braden had acted correctly. They argued that the American Ambassador had not told Argentines how to vote, that he had merely explained the feeling of the American government toward the current Argentine administration, that he had spoken for the United Nations in condemning the pro-Axis attitude of the Farrell-Perón group. One opposition political leader told the present author that he thought that Braden would go down in history as one of the best friends Argentina ever had.

Some foreign observers felt that the American error was not in having Braden attack the Farrell-Perón regime so strongly, but in having him leave so early. They felt that it would have been better for him to have stayed until after the election. They felt that if he had been present during the events of the October 9–17 period, the restoration of Perón would never have taken place. Braden, in their opinion, could have given opposition politicians the advice and the confidence they needed to take over the reigns of government in that fateful ten days.

With the consummation of October 17, the election campaign got under full steam. It was a bitter campaign, and the issue of "Braden o Perón" was a vibrant one throughout the whole contest. For the opposition, the connection of the Peronistas with the Nazis was also a telling issue, and it received aid from the United States with the publication of the famous Blue Book. In this document the conduct of the *de facto* Argentine government toward the war was subjected to long analysis, the names of the Nazis and Fascists to whom the Argentine regime had given refuge and protection were listed, and other acts of the Ramírez-Farrell-Perón regime, which the United States interpreted as favoring the Axis, were recorded for all to read.

The Blue Book was published just two weeks before the election, with the obvious intention of influencing the choice of the voters. In Washington, copies were handed by the Secretary of State to each ambassador from an American state. In Argentina the charges made in the Blue Book were given a great deal of publicity by the anti-Peronista press; they were repeated over and over again by Unión Democrática orators of all parties and in all parts of the land. However, the effect of the Blue Book is doubtful. Even some of those who felt that Braden's attacks on Perón were justified nevertheless argued that the publication of the Blue Book at that particular time did more to weaken than to strengthen the cause of the anti-Peronistas. Many of its charges were common discussion even before publication of the Blue Book, and their circulation at that particular moment by the United States government appeared to many to be undue interference in Argentine affairs. (This is not to say that the charges themselves were any less true.)

The Peronistas protested that, on the instigation of the United States, their country was being subjected to a virtual blockade by the United Nations. For some time after the war, most of the world's shipping continued to be regulated by the Anglo-American bodies set up for the purpose while the conflict was going on. The Argentines maintained that the curtailment of shipping to them was greatly in excess of the actual shipping shortage. Furthermore, the Argentine government, and Perón himself on various occasions, claimed that the Argentines found it impossible to purchase needed vehicles and other machinery which was available to other countries, but not to Argentina.

These charges undoubtedly have a certain degree of validity. Soon after the overthrow of General Ramírez it was announced that United States merchant ships would no longer stop at Buenos Aires, and although this type of boycott did not exist for more than a few months, there continued to be a marked reluctance on the part of the United States to deal with Argentina on an equal plane with other Latin American countries. Other moves intended to cripple Argentina economically were the freezing of gold deposits in the United States and a series of what were described by Sumner Welles as "minor and exasperating commercial restrictions."

The frigid atmosphere between Argentina and Tío Sam began to thaw immediately after the election of Juan Domingo Perón as president. On February 26, 1946, President Truman announced that George Messersmith would be sent as the new United States Ambassador to Argentina and that the United States was now willing to negotiate a hemisphere defense treaty with *all* the American republics. With Messersmith to Buenos Aires went a completely new policy toward the Argentine regime. Typical of the change was the fact that, far from branding Perón and his friends as pro-Nazi, Ambassador Messersmith even insisted that the Perón regime was not a dictatorship.

With the arrival of Ambassador Messersmith the change in atmosphere around the American Embassy was notable. Those who had been most active in befriending the opposition (such as the Cultural Attaché, John Griffiths) were summarily dismissed. The open door into the offices of the Ambassador and his chief aides, which had existed for the anti-Peronistas and the rank and file Argentines in general, was slammed shut.

There began an influx of American businessmen who thought that they saw profits to be made in Perón's economic development program. One of the first of these was a Louisiana shipbuilder who had skyrocketed to fame and fortune during the Second World War, Mr. Andrew Jackson Higgins. He attended Perón's inauguration on June 4, 1946, and upon his return to the United States was very vociferous in his attacks on what had hitherto been the policy of his country toward Perón. He was followed by many others, including George E. Allen, a former close associate of President Truman. Allen was reported to have come down to close a business deal with Ricardo Staudte, who had been denounced in the Blue Book as Argentina's Number Two Nazi. Allen stayed at the United States Embassy while he was in Argentina.

Other high American dignitaries also began to visit Argentina. Thus in December, 1948, New Mexico's Senator Dennis Chavez led a group of eight Congressmen on a pilgrimage to Buenos Aires. There, among other activities, they conferred with President Perón, and some expressed their admiration for the Perón administration.

Ambassador Messersmith was succeeded by Ambassador James Bruce, who went even farther than his predecessor in "appeasing" the Perón administration. At one time Ambassador Bruce addressed President Perón as "the great leader of a great nation." In summing up the drastic change which had occurred in the relations between the United States Embassy and the regime, under the guidance of Messrs. Messersmith and Bruce, the opposition newspaper *Reconstruir* in October, 1948, had this to say:

For every good Peronista it is an article of faith that Braden was a bad Yankee, representing the most odious imperialism, who came here with the mission of destroying our sovereignty and imposing the dominion of the oligarchy via the electoral victory of the Unión Democrática. But since the victory was won by the leader of the descamisados, good old Colonel Perón, the bad Yankee had to flee and was ignominiously removed from his post of Ambassador.

In his place came Mr. Messersmith and later Mr. Bruce, both of whom—and particularly the latter—were good friends of Perón. So good a friend is Mr. Bruce that he has not hesitated to return to his country to move heaven and earth to get Argentina included in the Marshall Plan. . . .

Mr. Bruce turns out then to be a good Yankee who works in favor of the consolidation of our economic independence. He even gives the impression of representing the government of Perón before that of Truman rather than the other way around.

The attitude of Perón in the face of this sudden veering in American policy was not a vacillating one. He would accept what the Yankees had to offer. (He is reported to have remarked to some of his more jittery aides during the height of the Braden onslaught: "Stay with me and don't worry. You will see that when the smoke all clears away, the Yankees will be down here with satchels trying to get orders from us." —and so they were.) However, Perón was not one to give the least impression of being sorry for past behavior or of kowtowing to the Americans in any way.

Indeed the Perón administration worked out an attitude in its relations with the United States which might almost be called diplomatic blackmail. The more the regime wanted economic aid of some kind from the United States, the more belligerent became the tone of the Peronista press and public figures. There are two notable instances of this: in the latter part of 1948 when the pinch of the dollar shortage really began to be felt in Argentina, and in the early part of 1950 when a loan was being negotiated with the Export-Import Bank.

Until the middle of 1948 the Argentines were riding along on the crest of the postwar demand for agricultural products. However, by that time the boom had begun to decline, and

Perón was finding it increasingly difficult to get dollars for the purchases which he wished to make in hard-currency countries. He had expected a great deal of profit to accrue to Argentina from the Marshall Plan (European Reconstruction Program, or E.R.P.), and had declared in numerous speeches his willingness to cooperate with the Plan on one condition—that Argentina be treated as an equal, not an inferior. Some of the Peronistas had been so bold as to intimate that one and a half billion of the first five billion dollars appropriated under E.R.P. would end up in Argentina for the purchase of foodstuffs.

They were disappointed for various reasons. They had overestimated the importance of food purchases under the Program, and had overlooked the provisions in the E.R.P. law which made mandatory purchases of goods in the United States, if they were available. Moreover, the policy of the Economic Cooperation Administration was to buy as little as possible in Argentina.

By the latter part of 1948 this disappointment had become acute. Foreign Minister Bramuglia is reported to have remarked, "I have been duped." Two measures were then taken. First, Ambassador Bruce was inveigled to go to Washington to see what he could do about getting a larger "cut" for Argentina under the Marshall Plan; and Perón and his friends launched a violent attack on the United States, crying loudly and often that Argentina did not need the help of any other power, that Argentina was as good as any other nation, and so on, *ad infinitum.*

These methods were not immediately successful. Argentine-American trade continued to fall. The *Foreign Commerce Weekly* of the United States Department of Commerce reported on December 5, 1949, that, in the first nine months of 1949, Argentina exported only $66 million worth of goods to the United States, compared with $153 million in the same period of the previous year, while the United States sold to Argentina only $100 million worth of goods, compared with $318 million the previous year.

About a year and a half later the Argentine tactics of bluff and bluster were repeated. This time, Assistant Secretary of State Edward Miller was on a tour of Latin America and passed through Argentina. It was widely rumored that he was there to discuss the possibilities of a loan, since Secretary of State Acheson had hinted that this was in the making. But Secretary Miller, upon his arrival, was greeted with the worst blast from the Peronista press that had been heard since the days of the "Braden o Perón" campaign. Indeed, that old campaign was brought out of mothballs, dusted off, and donned again for the edification of the Buenos Aires populace and Secretary Miller.

This violent campaign by *Democrácia, La Crítica, El Laborista, El Líder* and the hundred and one other pro-government newspapers was turned off as suddenly as it had been begun. After Secretary Miller had been there for a day or two, had conferred with the Foreign Minister Paz and with President Perón himself, the attacks on the United States were stopped and in their place were substituted soothing articles depicting the possibilities for eternal bliss in the future relations between Argentina and "our sister republic to the North."

It is not hard to guess just what had happened to bring about this sudden change of front on the part of the Peronista press. The upshot of the visit of Secretary Miller was the granting of a loan of $125 million to Argentina. The United States virtually apologized to Argentina for giving her the loan, not calling it a "loan" but rather a "grant," since Perón had not long since announced that he would accept no "loan" from any country. Furthermore, the "grant" was made not to the Argentine government, but to a number of private banks, with the Argentine government guaranteeing repayment. The purpose of the "grant" was to pay off accumulated commercial balances owed to American exporters.

Although, at the time, this "grant" of $125 million did not seem large enough to do more than stave off Argentina's economic crisis, it signified that our attitude toward Perón had swung around full circle. In December, 1945, Perón and his confrères were denounced by the United States as pro-Nazis and totalitarians; in May of 1950, they were being favored with multi-million dollar loans.

The startling quality of this about-face is further demonstrated by the fact that a Brazilian delegation seeking a grant of somewhat similar proportions had been waiting around Washington for six months, while Perón received his loan after only a few weeks (or was it that long?) of negotiation.

Just what were the motives for this complete change of heart toward Perón probably only the highest officials of the State Department know—and perhaps they are not quite sure. Certainly it was not because the Peronista leopard had changed its spots. The foregoing chapters of the present study have strongly indicated that the General's administration has been becoming increasingly totalitarian and has been systematically destroying the remnants of political democracy in the Argentine Republic.

Nor is the charge made by Braden, the Blue Book, and other official United States spokesmen, any less true today than it was five years ago. The Perón regime still harbors a large number of war criminals and other leading figures of the Nazi-dominated Europe of a decade ago. Leading Nazis, Fascists, and collaborators who have found refuge in Perón's Argentina include the following:

Vittorio Mussolini, son of Il Duce, who has quite openly engaged in Fascist propaganda in Argentina, and who pub-

licly commemorated the anniversary of the death of his father.

Carlo Scorza, long-time secretary of the Fascist Party, who
is living in Argentina under the name of Carlo Sartori, and at
one time was reported to be residing in a monastery.

General Mario Roata, one of Mussolini's top military officers, who is reputedly employed by Perón and is working in
the Casa Rosada, the Argentine White House.

Eduardo Moroni, one-time Minister of Agriculture of Mussolini, who is said to have a job with the Banco Central de la
Republica Argentina with a salary of six thousand pesos a
month.

A. Mutti, the last secretary of the Fascist Party under Mussolini.

Dino Grandi, for many years Mussolini's Foreign Minister
and later Italian Ambassador to Great Britain.

Fritz Mandl, Austrian Nazi who transferred much of his
European and industrial empire to Argentina, where he has
worked closely with Argentine officials in developing the Five
Year Plan.

Ludwig Freude, listed in the Blue Book as Nazi No. 1 in
Argentina, whose naturalized son has served as personal secretary to Perón and is reputed to be in charge of the regime's
secret police.

Ricardo Staudte, another leading Nazi industrialist, who
fled to Argentina before the end of the war; he is listed in the
Blue Book as Nazi No. 2 in Argentina.

Otto Skorzeny, SS leader and close associate of Hitler, who
makes his base of operations in Argentina, but travels back and
forth to Europe, where, he frankly admits, he is keeping the
Nazi underground machine in condition.

Admiral Litzman, ex-commander of the German Black Sea
Fleet.

Professor Willy Tank, a leading Nazi aircraft designer.

Generals Adolph Galland of the Luftwaffe and Baumback of the Wehrmacht.

Dr. H. Theiss and Messrs. F. Adam, H. Richner, and J. Paescht, ex-officials of the Gestapo, who are acting in an "advisory capacity" to the Argentine Federal Police Force.

Ante Pavelic, one-time president of the Nazi puppet state of Croatia.

José Figuerola, a one-time intimate of Primo de Rivera, Spanish Fascist predecessor of Franco in the 1920's; Figuerola has been economic adviser to Perón since the beginning of the Peronista regime and has been credited with drawing up the Five Year Plan.

Numerous smaller fry from all over Fascist Europe have found refuge in Peronista Argentina. Radical Deputy Silvano Santander, who first revealed the presence of Otto Skorzeny in Argentina, claimed that thirty other ranking German Nazis were also there. In March, 1949, two Quisling leaders sought by the Norwegian government were reported as having reached Argentina.

Thus, a changed attitude by Perón toward Fascism certainly cannot be a reason for the complete shift in the United States attitude toward Perón. It seems likely that the cold war has been the major consideration. Perón has the most powerful air force in Latin America, one of the most powerful armies, the largest merchant fleet, and a navy of not unimportant tonnage. Hence, it might be argued that Perón would be a dangerous antagonist to United States but a valuable ally in the event of a Third World War. So, it is reasoned, the United States must buy Perón's services.

There seems to be just one hitch in this reasoning. That is that Perón is not for sale. He will take what the United States has to offer, and then come back and ask for more, threatening that if the more is not forthcoming, he will "go over to the other side." However, he is very unlikely to carry out any such

threat. Perón is smart enough to know that whatever ambitions he has for hegemony over South America would come
to naught if Russia won the "cold" war or its "hot" successor.
As early as 1946, Perón stated that in case of a showdown
he would be on the side of the United States.

Nevertheless, it is undoubtedly true that the United States
armed forces have been one of the groups most anxious to
reach an "understanding" with Perón. As early as 1944 a two-
man delegation consisting of Roving Ambassador Avra War-
ren and Air Force General George Brett visited Argentina.
They reached an over-all agreement with the regime on military, aviation, and economic problems. This agreement was
negated, however, by subsequent developments. Since then,
visits back and forth between the military of the two countries
have continued, regardless of the relationship between their
governments. In 1948 General Perón conferred the Order of
the Liberator San Martín upon seven United States generals,
and also upon Admiral Denfield and General Harry Vaughan,
President Truman's military aide. Later that year, one hundred Argentine Air Force cadets came to the United States to
tour and train at this country's Air Force installations. There is
little doubt that our armed forces have had a great deal to do
with the softening of our policy toward Perón.

Important, too, have been United States businessmen
(many of them with close connections with the Truman administration), who have sought to carry on business with
Argentina and make what they could out of the economic
development program of the Perón regime. Ambassador
Bruce himself was a businessman by profession, while Ambassador Messersmith had close contacts with business interests.

Moreover, an important element inside the State Department was opposed to the Braden policies and tried hard to
soften the attitude of the United States. One of the leaders of

this element was Sumner Welles, a professional diplomat for most of his adult life, and Assistant Secretary and Under Secretary of State for many years. Although Welles left the Department in 1943, his opinion undoubtedly was shared by many of his colleagues, and when Braden was ousted from the Department, they could make their weight felt.

Undoubtedly the thinking of these diplomats was influenced by the very unhappy effect—from the point of view of Latin American–United States relations—which the Braden policy had on the other Latin American nations. To many Latin Americans the Braden incident looked like the revival of strong-arm diplomacy, of intervention in the internal affairs of another American republic. United States citizens who do not want to see the revival of the Big Stick were also made uneasy by this approach—and even more so by its failure.

No matter what the faults of Braden's policy, one thing certainly seems clear—that his successors went too far in the other direction. A strong case can be made *against* a United States Ambassador who virtually asks the people of the country to which he is accredited to overthrow their government. An equally strong case can perhaps be made *for* having at least formally friendly relations with the accredited government—in this case the Perón regime.

There would seem but little justification, however, for going as far as the United States did after February 24, 1946. This country almost completely snubbed the democratic elements in Argentina (with whom its natural affinity certainly lies), while going almost as far in supporting Perón as Braden had gone in opposing him. We capped it with a loan to get Perón out of his economic difficulties—to be followed by how many other loans?

The people of Argentina are agreed that, if anything will bring down the Perón administration, it will be an economic crisis. Although it perhaps is not right for the United States to precipitate such a crisis, or to urge the people to oust their government, neither is it necessary for the United States to offer help to Perón's regime out of the economic morass into which it has gotten itself.

Early in 1951 there was some indication that the United States attitude toward Argentina might be undergoing still another change. Assistant Secretary of State Miller formally expressed United States' concern over the suppression of *La Prensa*, though the United States delegation to the Inter-American Foreign Ministers Conference held in Washington in March, 1951, saw to it that the subject was not raised there. The appointment as the new American Ambassador to Buenos Aires of Ellsworth Bunker, a man of known liberal tendencies, also gave some hope that the attitude of the United States Embassy there might be a little less cool toward the anti-Peronistas and a little less intent on appeasing "El Líder."

POST SCRIPTUM

⸙

THE PERÓN ERA promises to alter the whole course of Argentine history. The government of General Juan Domingo Perón is something more than the run-of-the-mill Latin American strong-arm regime. It is a totalitarian administration which not only demands that the citizen must submit to its high-handed conduct of public affairs, but must give active demonstration of support.

Slowly but surely all phases of Argentine life are being made to conform to the Peronista model. The trade unions have been converted into little more than a tool of the government. The worker is being taught that he cannot reach out and try to make economic and social gains on his own account, but must accept only what "El Líder," "Evita," and the rest of the gang see fit to give him. An independent trade union movement is anathema in the Argentina of President-General Juan Domingo Perón.

All phases of economic life are being brought within a single strait-jacket. The export of basic crops is converted into a tool for the ambitions and the policies of the ruling clique. The nation's wheat and corn growers, cattle raisers and shepherds are thus put completely under the power of the ruling group in the "just" regime of "El Líder."

The industrialists, too, are meeting the same fate. Industrialization is being carried out under completely political control and much of it under actual military control. All independent organizations of Argentine industrialists have been either "intervened" or otherwise forced to conform. Individual anti-Perón industrialists, such as the chemical magnate Massone, have been forced to take refuge in Montevideo.

All means of communication and discussion are being made mere mouthpieces for the regime. The great radio stations of Buenos Aires and the provinces have been forced by subornation, purchase, or intimidation to become cogs in the wheel of the Peronista propaganda machine. All newspapers, with but one exception, have been forced either to become part of the propaganda apparatus or to go underground. The great motion picture industry—which was one of the prides of Argentina—has become but one more weapon in the armory of the Peronista politicos.

Nor have the great social and political institutions of the country escaped this all-encompassing totalitarian trend. The Catholic Church was first inveigled into a compromising position of political support of the regime, and then found itself helpless to withdraw from this alliance.

The Army seems to have been purged of all those who might question or be jealous of the authority of the Dictator and his friends. Militarism is entering into every phase of the country's public life. Military men hold civilian positions— elected and appointive—in great profusion. A large segment of the nation's economy has been placed under the direct control of the Ministry of Defense. By means of large appropriations, munificent salaries, and greatly heightened prestige within the nation, the Armed Forces have been bribed into acquiescence and cooperation with the Peronista rulers.

Education is confounded with propaganda. From infancy, Argentine children are now being taught that their nation's history virtually began with Juan Domingo Perón, and that anyone who does not agree completely with the policies, ideas, and institutions of the Peronista state is a traitor to the nation and to humanity itself. "Loyalty checks" by political Federal Police are demanded of teachers and students alike. All faculty members, whether in primary, secondary, or higher schools, whose allegiance to Peronismo is in the least open to question, have been ousted.

The checks and balances of a political democracy are being steadily eliminated. Not only does the Peronista group refuse to seat some of the elected opposition members, but it cavalierly ousts from their posts as the people's representatives those leaders of the opposition whom it considers too dangerous. The Supreme Court has been converted into a Peronista tool, by means of a wholesale purge; lesser judicial bodies have received similar treatment.

Thus, though the average visitor to Buenos Aires probably is not at all aware of the spreading pall of the totalitarianism which is slowly but nonetheless completely blacking out the cultural diversity, the vigorous market of ideas, and the democratic spirit which have made Argentina one of the great nations of the hemisphere, the process is nonetheless moving relentlessly on.

The nature of Argentine totalitarianism leads to much confusion among outside observers. On the one hand, there are those Liberals who, because they have labeled the Argentine regime as "Fascist," cannot see that the basis of Perón's support among the people of Argentina is the program of social and economic reform he pursued in the middle years of the 1940's. These Liberals pronounce his social legislation as nothing more than "demagoguery," and refuse to admit that he really received the backing of the great mass of the leadership and the membership of the country's trade union movement. The Liberals are willing enough to believe that Perón is converting the trade union movement into a species of Labor Front—which is true—but they are not willing to admit that he was in a position to do so only because that same labor movement was responsible for keeping him in power, once the Army had put him there—which is also true.

It was this same lack of appreciation of Perón's program which led the opposition to underestimate the influence he had gained in the ranks of the workers. The Radicals and Socialists, who make up the bulk of the opposition to Perón, did not understand until it was too late that Perón really had done things which the workers felt were in their interest and which therefore won him their gratitude and loyalty. The opposition has now awakened to this fact, but it may be too late, despite the gallantry and heroism of the anti-Peronista forces.

On the other hand there are those—and many of them are found in high places—who refuse to recognize the totalitarian nature of the Peronista regime. Because it has until recently allowed the two papers *La Nación* and *La Prensa* to continue publication, because there *is* still a Congress with a number of opposition deputies sitting in Buenos Aires, because Perón *has* carried out a program of economic development and social reform which is commendable, this group fails to recognize, or at least to admit, that the Peronista regime is nonetheless dangerous.

This group, many of whose members seem to be in the State Department, the halls of the United States Congress, and in other positions of trust, therefore continues to treat the Argentine regime as if it were one more Good Neighbor. It carries "appeasement" to the extreme of advocating—and then granting—loans to Perón's Argentina. It seems to overlook the extensive work of propaganda and subversion which Perón and his friends are conducting in other Latin American countries. It seems to refuse to believe in the possibility that Perón may succeed in his cherished aim of forming a Latin American bloc independent of and defiant of the United States.

Not all the people in this second group are to be found in the United States. The British, for instance, for long overlooked the totalitarian implications of the Peronista regime. All too many Latin American politicians and labor leaders notice only the labor legislation Perón has put on the books, or his success in defying the United States, and do not see the dangers which the Peronista movement and administration augur for themselves and their countries.

It is high time that people in both these camps took another look at the Peronista administration as it really is. If the Liberals want to call Perón "fascist," that is well and good. However, they should recognize the nature of the appeal which he has made. They should realize the implications of the fact that the people of once-proud Argentina were willing to sell their liberty for supposed economic and social benefits. This is the real lesson of Argentina's experience for the Liberals.

On the other hand, the statesmen of Latin America should come to realize without equivocation that although Perón may be successful in defying the United States, he has also been eminently successful in wiping out civil liberty and economic, social, and political freedom within the borders of Argentina. They should remember that Perón was the leader of the brutally imperialist-minded Grupo de Oficiales Unidos, which made little secret of its desire to dominate the South American continent and impose upon it a concentration camp regime patterned on those of Hitler's Europe. Nor should they forget the economic treaties which Perón offered his neighbors in the first flush of exuberance in 1946 and 1947: treaties which would have gone far toward destroying what economic independence those nations now enjoy and, in the long run, subverting their political independence as well.

North Americans, too, should be wide-awake to the dangers of Perón and his regime. Perón's Argentina is the spearhead of the reactionary dictatorial bloc among American nations.

This bloc has no regard for the political democracy and freedom for which the United States stands in the world. Under Argentine leadership this bloc seeks to destroy the still-remaining democracies in the Western Hemisphere. Unless the United States is careful, she will one day wake up to find a united front of totalitarian military dictatorships among the nations to the South, proudly headed and dominated by El Líder—Su Excelencia Señor Presidente de la Republica Argentina, General Juan Domingo Perón.

BIBLIOGRAPHICAL NOTE

❧❧❧

MUCH OF THE BASIC INFORMATION for this volume was collected by the author while visiting Argentina late in 1946, gathering data for a history of the country's labor movement. He visited several provincial cities as well as Buenos Aires, and talked with labor leaders and political figures in all of the principal political groups. He talked with leading Peronista legislators and government officials, as well as with leaders of the Radical and Socialist opposition parties, the Communists, and Cipriano Reyes's Laboristas.

During this visit, the author talked over labor problems and labor history with leaders of many of the most important unions in the country. These included figures in Peronista unions such as the Unión Ferroviaria, La Fraternidad, Unión Tranviaria, the Packinghouse Workers Federation, the Buenos Aires Printing Trades Workers, and Peronista unions of maritime workers, metal workers, construction workers, bank employees, commercial employees, and a variety of others. He also talked to anarchist and syndicalist unions, such as the F.O.R.A., the Unión Sindical Argentina, the Shipbuilders Federation, and the Unión Sindical Marítima; and with the leaders of the Socialist-controlled shoemakers and textile workers unions.

The information and impressions gathered on this trip were supplemented by various other sources, such as the report of the American Federation of Labor delegation which visited Argentina in January, 1947, and by various books. Two of the best of the latter are Ray Josephs's *Argentine Diary* (Random House, 1944), and Ruth and Leonard Greenup's *Revolution before Breakfast* (University of North Carolina, 1947).

226   BIBLIOGRAPHICAL NOTE

Interesting information concerning the background of the
Peronista drive for power is contained in Felix Weil's *Argentine
Riddle* (John Day, 1944), written by an Argentine-born son of an
important pre-Hitler German exporter to Argentina who has had
considerable experience in Argentine politics and academic life.

Another valuable source of background information is José
Figuerola's *La Colaboración Social en Hispanoamerica* (Editorial
Sudamericana, Buenos Aires, 1943). Figuerola, a former associate
of Spanish dictator Primo de Rivera, has been one of Perón's
chief economic advisers; he outlines in this book the kind of a
corporate state he would like to build in Latin America, and also
gives important information on the status of social legislation and
the labor movement before the June 4, 1943, Revolution. Perón
himself has contributed something in this field by a pamphlet
published in Buenos Aires in 1948 entitled "Political and Social
Situation Prior to the Revolution of 1943."

For information on Argentine labor history a number of sources
are valuable. There exist published histories of several leading
Argentine unions, including La Fraternidad and the telephone
workers. General histories of labor have been written by Jacinto
Oddone, a Socialist, and Diego Abad de Santillán, a Spanish anarchosyndicalist. The most recent work of this nature is Juan C.
Juárez's *Los Trabajadores en Función Social* (Ateneo de Estudios
Sociales, Buenos Aires, 1947), written from a Peronista point of
view and containing much interesting information on the unions
organized under Perón's auspices.

Much of the information contained in the present book has
come from Argentine newspapers and periodicals, of both Peronista
and anti-government orientation. Among the Peronista publications which the author has found most useful have been *C.G.T.*,
the organ of the Confederación General del Trabajo; *Unión
Tranviaria Automotor,* organ of the trolley-car and bus drivers
union; and *Hechos e Ideas.* The last is a monthly magazine which
is the spokesman for those Radicals who joined the Peronista
camp. It has interesting articles concerning economic as well as
political developments in Perón's Argentina.

Anti-Peronista Argentine publications which have been particularly useful include the Socialist paper *La Vanguardia* and its various successors *El Socialista, La Lucha,* and *Nuevas Bases.* The illegal edition of *La Vanguardia,* which ceased appearing early in 1950, was a particularly good source of information.

Other very useful anti-Peronista periodicals are *Argentina Libre,* published in Uruguay by Argentine exiles, and *Reconstruir,* published by an anarchosyndicalist group called the Unión Socialista Libertaria, also printed in Montevideo but widely distributed in Argentina as well as abroad. Another anarchist paper of less value is the *Acción Libertaria* published by the more orthodox Federación Anarquista Argentina.

For general day-to-day information on Argentine developments, the New York *Times* is invaluable, while for Argentine labor developments the publications of various international labor groups are frequently very useful. Of particular interest in this connection are the *Information Bulletin* of the International Confederation of Free Trade Unions; the *Inter-American Labor Notes,* published by the AFL-backed Inter-American Confederation of Workers; and the *Noticiero Obrero Latinoamericano,* put out by the Communist-controlled Confederación de Trabajadores de América Latina. In a somewhat similar category is "Hemispherica," the monthly publication of the United States Committee of the Inter-American Association for Democracy and Freedom.

An important source of information concerning the stated doctrines and boasted accomplishments of the Perón administration is a series of pamphlets written by Perón and published in 1948. These included the following titles:

"The Argentine International Policy"
"Political Course of the Future"
"The Economic Reform"
"Social Reform"
"Nuestro Petroleo"
"La Obra del Gobierno y la Labor Destructiva Gradual de los que Intentan Alterar el Orden"

A number of other interesting pamphlets have been issued by the Peronistas to explain various parts of their program and actions.

228   BIBLIOGRAPHICAL NOTE

Among those which the present author has consulted have been the following:

"Doctrinary Principles of the Social Policy of His Excellency the President of the Republic General Juan Perón" (Buenos Aires, 1947)

"Los Ferrocarriles Son Argentinos" (Buenos Aires, 1948)

"Declaraciones sobre la Economía Argentina formuladas en Conferencia de Prensa por el Dr. Ramón A. Cereijo, Ministro de Hacienda de la Nación" (Buenos Aires, 1948)

"Perón Cumple Su Plan de Gobierno" (Buenos Aires, 1948)

"El General Perón examina el actual Política Economica Argentina"

"Como Fué Despojado el Colono Argentino"—outline of Peronista agrarian reform program and previous conditions

"Justicia Social en el Campo Argentino"—Peronista agrarian program

"Conferencia del General Perón con los Legisladores Nacionales" (Buenos Aires, 1948)

"Perón pone fin a la carrera de precios y salarios" (Buenos Aires, 1947)

"Radiografia Politica del General Perón" by Eduardo García.

The Confederación General del Trabajo has published a number of Peronista pamphlets, including a description of the events of October 17: "17 de Octubre—Jornada Heroica del Pueblo y para el Pueblo" (1947). The C.G.T. also put out a pamphlet on the 1946 election entitled "Comicios Ejemplares" (1946), and one condemning the sugar workers' strike of December 1949 entitled "La Traición de los dirigentes de la FOTIA y la FEIA a los trabajadores del Azucar" (1949). The author has found all of these pamphlets very useful in the preparation of the present volume.

Considerable light is thrown on the economic policies of Perón by a publication of the Department of Economic Affairs of the United Nations entitled *Economic Development in Selected Countries*, published in October, 1947. Another useful source of information on current Peronista economic policies is the London weekly *The Economist* which has been frequently cited in these pages. Carleton Beals's *Lands of the Dawning Morrow* (Bobbs Merrill, 1948) has a very sympathetic discussion of Perón's agrarian and economic programs.

The chapters on Argentina's relations with other countries have depended a great deal on information contained in Sumner Welles's *Where Are We Heading?* (Harper & Bros., 1946), and *The Memoirs of Cordell Hull,* published for the former Secretary of State by Macmillan in 1948. Of great use in this connection, also, was a recent Brazilian volume, Mario Martins's *Peron—um Confronto entre Argentina e o Brasil* (Edicões do Povo, Rio de Janeiro, 1950). Martins's book is also a valuable source of information concerning other aspects of the Perón regime, including its suppression of civil liberties, Peronista militarism, and the Perón government's economic program.

Many of the sources of information noted here are not available to the general American reading public. However, the author hopes that he has made discreet and careful use of these materials and that the present volume will leave the reader with as rounded a picture of the Perón Era as is possible in the comparatively few pages which we have devoted to it.

INDEX

Act of Chapultepec, 202
Adaro, Dalmiro, 61
Aged, the, rights of, under the new constitution, 80
Agrarian reform, program of, 143 ff.
Agricultural products, government monopoly, 148 ff.; low prices to farmers, 149; decline in production, 150; increase in prices to farmers, 150; high prices of, protested by other countries, 180
Agricultural workers, conditions of, 141 f.
Aguirre, Carlos Antonio, 96
Airforce, 119, 121; expansion of, 214 f.
Air lines, expansion of, 162 f.
Albariño, Ramón Amancio, 116
Aliens, constitutional provisions re naturalization, 82
Allen, George E., 208
Alvarez, Juan, 37
Alvear, de, Marcelo T., 3
Anarchist unions, 86 f.
Andes Convention, 178 f.
Andrea, de, Miguel, 89, 129 f.
Anti-Semitism, 135
Aprista Party, 189
Argaña, José, 23
Argentina, relations with Russia, 72, 174, 215; international relations under Perón, 170-86; relations with Spain, 171 ff.; relations with the United States, 176; break with Axis powers, 199; United States memorandum re Farrell regime,

200 f.; withdrawal of foreign ambassadors to, 201; accord with United States, 203; pro-Axis attitude, 205; grievances re postwar shipping, 206 f.; assets frozen by the United States, 207; influx of American businessmen, 208, 215; economic straits after 1948, 210 ff.; 1950 "grant" from the United States, 212
Argentina Libre, 63
Argentine Industrial Union, 33
Argentine Regional Labor Federation (F.O.R.A.), 86
Argentine Rural Confederation, 33
Argentine Rural Society, 33
Army, revolution of 1930, 4; revolution of 1943, 3 ff., 12-19, 115; German-trained officers, 14; and October 17, 1945, 33 ff.; power vis-à-vis civilians increased under new constitution, 78; political importance under Perón, 115-24; salary scale of officers, 118; modernization and budget, 119 ff.; control of public life, 219
Asquia, Miel, 112
Avalos, Eduardo J., 35 f.; resignation, 40

Bahía Blanca, 61
Balbín, Ricardo, 68 f.
Banco Central, nationalized, 156 f.; restriction on credit, 164
Banco de Crédito Industrial Argentino, 161

234 INDEX

Foreign trade, agreements re, 177 ff.; subsidized by Argentina, 181 f.; decline after 1948, 210 ff.

France, Eva Perón's visit to, 107

Franco, Francisco, and Perón, 172 ff.

Fraternidad, La, 8, 15, 29

Fresco, Manuel, 5

Freire, José María, 107

Freude, Ludwig, 213

Fundación Ayuda Social María Eva Duarte de Perón, 107 ff., 126

Gainza Paz, Alberto, 34

Galland, Adolph, 214

Gallegos, Rómulo, 196

García, Enrique Eduardo, re Perón and Irigoyen, 44

Gay, Luis, 30, 43, 57, 91, 110

General Confederation of Labor, (C.G.T.), 9; split in ranks, 10; No. 1, 16; No. 2, 15, 30; and Perón, 28 ff., 92; control over affiliated unions, 85, 91; and Eva Perón, 110 f.; delegation to International Confederation of Free Trade Unions in Mexico City, 192; pamphlets, 228

Genta, Bruno, 134 ff.

Gentille, Armando G., 43

Ghioldi, Américo, 11

Ghioldi, Rodolfo, 50

González, Joaquin V., 133

G.O.U., see Grupo de Officiales Unidos

Government, structural changes in, under the new constitution, 77

Government control, over transportation, 76; extension of, under new constitution, 81 f.; over unions (see also under Interventor), 85; over economic affairs, 155 ff.; in all areas of Argentine life, 218-23

Government monopoly, of purchase and sale of agricultural products, 148 ff.

Governors, provincial, military men among, 115 f.

Grafa Company, strike, 26

Grandi, Dino, 213

Great Britain, railroads owned in and sold to Argentina, 157 f.; Argentina liquidates its debt to, 158 f.; trade agreements with Argentina, 178 ff.

Greenup, Ruth and Leonard, *Revolution before Breakfast*, 225

Gregorio, Candido, 90

Griffiths, John, 58 f., 128, 207

Grupo de Officiales Unidos (G.O.U.), 12 ff., 195

Haiti, Perón's labor attaché in, 191

Havana, International Trade Organization, 176; Perón's labor attaché in, 191

Hechos e Ideas, 226

Hemispherica, 131 f.

Hernández, Aurelio, 110 f.

Hora, La, 72, 74

Higgins, Andrew Jackson, 208

Housing, low-cost, 24

Houssay, Bernardo, 137

Hull, Cordell, *Memoirs*, 229

I.A.P.I., see Instituto Argentino de Producción e Intercambio

Iberluccea, Enrique, 11

I.C.F.T.U., see International Confederation of Free Trade Unions

Immigration of workers, 7 f.

Imports, restrictions on, 182 f.

Industrialization, 117; under the Five Year Plan, 159 f.; political and military control of, 218 f.

Industry, subsidized, 165

Inflation, measures to combat, 163 ff.; causes of, 167 f.

Instituto Argentino de Producción e Intercambio (I.A.P.I.), 148 ff.

Inter-American Development Bank, 177

International Confederation of Free Trade Unions (I.C.F.T.U.), 90; meeting in Mexico City, 192

International conferences, Peronista delegations, 194 f.

International Labor Organization, 188

International trade, Anglo-American postwar regulation of, 206

States, 174; message to the world,
174 f.; role in international conferences, 176 f.; use of economic pressure against other Latin American
countries, 184 ff.; denial of imperialistic ambitions, 185 f.; use of labor attachés to spread Peronismo,
187-97; conferral of Order of the
Liberator San Martín on U.S. generals, 215; pamphlets written by,
226, 227
Perón, María Eva Duarte de, 103-15;
purchases *Noticias Gráfica*, 64; re
railroad workers strike in 1951,
98 f.; Welfare Foundation, 107 ff.,
126; gift of garments to needy children of Washington, D.C., 108;
urged for public office, 113 f.; and
the army, 122 f.; gift to Costa Rica,
190
Peronismo, attempts to win Latin
American converts to, 187-97
"Personería gremial," 31 f.
Peru, Confederation of Workers vs.
Perón's labor attaché in, 189 f.; la-
bor leaders and Odría, 192 f.
Peso, devaluation of, 183
Peter, José, 100
Picconi, Luis Dante, 28
Pistarini, Juan, 4, 40
Political parties, in the 1945–46 cam-
paign, 43 ff.; legislation vs., 69
Porteños, 22
Pound sterling, devaluation of, 182
Prensa, La, 34; battle with Perón,
62 ff., 99; nationalized, 68; in 1949
strike, 95; U.S. concern over sup-
pression of, 217
Presidential campaign, 1945–46, 42 ff.
Press, suppression of, 17, 62-68
Price controls, 165 f.
Price increases, 167
Prices, of Argentina's products, pro-
tested by other countries, 180
Principios, Los, 66
Printing trades workers, 88 f.
Private property, right to, 81
Production, 167; industrial, decline
in, 163 f.

Prostitution, Perón vs. the Church
over legalization of, 131
Provincias Unidos, 63
Public office, qualifications for, 83
Public officials, Evita's influence re,
111 ff.
Public schools, Catholic religious in-
struction in, 17, 126; Peronista
propaganda in, 132
Pueblo, El, 66
Pueblo Unido, 74

Quijano, Hortensio, 43

Radical Party, *see* Unión Civica Radi-
cal
Radio broadcasting, Peronista at-
tempts to influence, 193 f.
Railroads, strikes, 1950–51, 97 f.; na-
tionalization of, 157 f.
Ramírez, Pedro P., 4; vs. Castillo,
12 f.; resignation as president, 18
— regime: pro-Axis, 15 ff.; oppres-
sive measures, 16-19; opposition to,
33; recognized by U.S., 199
Rawson, Arturo, 14
Razón, La, 34, 63
Reconstruir, 208 f.
Reforestation, 161
Rent and Sharecropping Law, 146
Repetto, Nicolás, 11, 15, 49
Reyes, Cipriano, 38, 94; vs. Peronismo, 54 ff.; plot to assassinate
Perón, 128
Roata, Mario, 213
Rodriguez Araya, charges vs. I.A.P.I.,
68, 151
Roman Catholic Church, religious in-
struction in the public schools, 17,
126; re party candidates, 127 f.;
and labor, 131; Peronistas attempts
to gain support of clergy, 194; *see
also* Church and State
Rural workers, *see* Agricultural work-
ers

Saadi, Vicente, 129
Salamon, Ricardo, 66
Sammartino, Ernesto Enrique, 68

San Martín, governor of Córdoba, 116
Santa Fe (prov.), 61
Santa Fe, University of, *see* Universidad del Litoral
Santander, Silvano, 214
Scorza, Carlo, 213
Secratariat of Labor and Social Welfare, 24
Sharecroppers, 146
Shipbuilding Workers, Federation of, 87
Shipping, 162
Shoe Workers Union, National, 31 f.
Siege, state of, 33 ff., 204; suspension of constitutional guarantees, 70 f.; under the new constitution, 78
Skorzeny, Otto, 213
Small farmers, 142 ff.
Socialist Party, 3 ff.; union leadership, 9; and labor, 11; vs. Perón, 63; leaders of the opposition, 71
Social legislation, in the new constitution, 79-81; for rural workers, 145 f.; basis of popular support of Perón, 221
Social security, 24
Solari, Juan Antonio, 11, 119
Sosa Molina, Humberto, 39, 121
Spain, Eva Perón's visit to, 106 f.; relations with Argentina, 171 ff.
Standard of living, 168 f.
State ownership, areas of, 81 f.
Statute of the Peon, 144
Staudte, Ricardo, 208, 213
Steel industry, 162
Stettinius, Edward, 200
Strike, right of, 80
Strikes, Grafa Company, Perón's attitude toward, 26; students, 35; general, 1945, 38 ff.; taxicab drivers, 86 ff.; packinghouse workers and others, 93 ff.; sugar workers, 96, 108
Students, opposition to Ramírez regime, 18 f.; strike, 1945, 35; opposition to Perón's regime, 133 ff.; political campaigning, 136
Subsidies, 164 f., 181 f.
Sugar plantations, 143

Sugar Workers, Federation of, 27; strike, 1949, 96, 108
Supreme Court, purged in 1946, 62; qualifications for membership, 83; a Peronista tool, 220
Sustaito, R., 36

Tamborini, José P., 45
Tank, Willy, 213
Taxicab Drivers Union, strike, 1946, 86
Teisaire, Alberto, 116, 121
Telephone system, nationalized, 157
Telephone Workers, Federation of, 30, 91
Tenant farmers, 146
Textile Workers Union, 31 f.
Tixi Massa, 195
Torino, Michel, 148
Trade agreements, bilateral, 183
Trade barriers, to protect industries of backward countries, 176
Trade union, *see* Union, labor
Transportation, expansion of, 162
Transport Workers Federation, International, 87
Treaties, economic, with neighboring countries, 184
Truman, Harry S., 207
Tucumán (prov.), 27; strike, 1949, 96 f.
Tucumán, University of, 133

Unión, La, 129
Union, labor, factors favoring growth of, 7 ff.; Ramírez vs., 15 f.; Perón's early fostering of, 22-32; political rise of leaders under Perón, 30 f.; anti-Peronista, 33, 54 ff., 85 ff., 94 ff., 99 f.; Eva Perón and, 104 ff., 107 ff.
Unión Cívica Radical, 3 ff., 63; support of Perón for president, 43; presidential campaign, 1945-46, 46 ff.; and the Labor Party, 55; election in 1946, 61; deputies expelled for "disrespect," 68; leaders of the opposition, 70; opposition in